100 KILLER LICKS
& CHOPS FOR
ROCK GUITAR

100 KILLER LICKS & CHOPS FOR ROCK GUITAR

THE LICKS & CHOPS YOU NEED—AND HOW TO USE THEM—FOR COOL, INTENSE ROCK

PHIL CAPONE

CHARTWELL
BOOKS, INC.

This edition published in 2009 by Chartwell Books, Inc.
a division of Book Sales, Inc.
276 Fifth Avenue Suite 206,
New York,
New York 10001,
USA

ISBN-10: 0-7858-2488-X
ISBN-13: 978-0-7858-2488-6
QTT.ROG

This book was conceived, designed, and produced by
Quintet Publishing Limited
The Old Brewery
6 Blundell Street
London N7 9BH
United Kingdom

Project Editor: Robert Davies
Designer: Steve West
Art Director: Michael Charles
Managing Editor: Donna Gregory
Publisher: James Tavendale

Printed in China by Midas Printing International Ltd.

9 8 7 6 5 4 3 2 1

CONTENTS

INTRODUCTION

Many questions face the aspiring rock guitarist: Where to begin? Which players to listen to? How did they create their sound? What effects did they use? What scales did they use to create their licks and riffs?

This book aims to answer all those questions through an in-depth analysis of the playing styles of the greatest guitarists the world has seen since the birth of rock music. Work through this book and you'll be a vastly different player by the time you've finished it—fully schooled up and ready to rock like a pro. It's no secret that the guitar heroes of each generation have drawn on a broad range of influences to create their own distinctive styles. They all listened to music that had come before, learned how it worked, and absorbed its influence into their own style to make something new and exciting. Developing an individual style is something we all crave, but it's impossible without exploring a wide range of styles. Don't forget that all the great guitarists have one thing in common—a recognition and understanding of the musicians that preceded them.

You don't need to be a guitar whizz to use this book, but a functional level of ability is assumed. Players of all levels should find it a useful and informative resource. Because this is not a traditional "teach yourself" book, it is not progressive; it can be dipped into at any point—whenever inspiration or just some fresh ideas are needed. All the licks and riffs are demonstrated on the accompanying CD so don't be put off by "the dots." As long as you can read TAB (and we've even included an explanation in case you can't), you'll be able to play everything in this book. An extensive scales and chops section follows the lick chapters to help you to improve your technique and increase your knowledge of the fingerboard.

There are of course many tuition books and DVDs on the market today. But this product is genuinely unique. It illustrates the stylistic approaches of as many pioneering guitarists as we could squeeze in, from the earliest rock & roll to grunge and beyond. As well as learning some cool riffs, licks, and chops, you're getting a comprehensive history of rock guitar. So what are you waiting for? Crank up that amp—let's rock!

HOW TO USE THIS BOOK

KILLER LICKS

These boxes provide essential information on technique, as well as suggesting when to use each lick.

Play the relevant track on the CD to hear how the lick should sound.

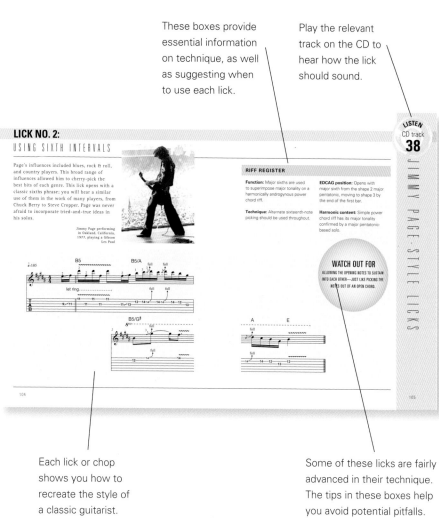

Each lick or chop shows you how to recreate the style of a classic guitarist.

Some of these licks are fairly advanced in their technique. The tips in these boxes help you avoid potential pitfalls.

SCALES AND CHOPS

The scales and chops section is the "technique busting" part of the book designed to advance your playing skills. Instead of just ascending and descending stepwise scale patterns, these challenging exercises will prepare you for "real world" improvisation scenarios.

CHOP NO. 1:
THE MINOR PENTATONIC

Scale Type: 5-note, minor

Formulae: R–b3–4–5–b7–Oct

Usage: Tonic minor scale that can also be superimposed over dominant and major chords.

Characteristics: Although this is a minor scale, rock musicians have been forcing it over major and dominant seventh chords since the early days of rock & roll—a technique borrowed from the blues pioneers. The minor third and minor seventh are frequently played slightly sharp by applying quarter-tone bends, regardless of what chord type the scale is played over.

Practice Notes: All five shapes for the scale are given here in A minor. The scale should be practiced in all keys. To maximize your fluency in each shape, try moving simple licks from shape one to the remaining four shapes. Root notes have been highlighted in each shape with an "R" between the staves. These "target notes" are essential for creating effective licks.

Each scale is accompanied by informative text that explains the notes in each scale and which chords you can play it over. Tips for maximizing practice are included to fast track your progress.

Each exercise is presented clearly and concisely using conventional notation and TAB. Helpful fingering suggestions are also provided to eliminate awkward or clumsy hand movements.

HISTORY OF ROCK

Rock music and the electric guitar are inseparable. In 1950, Fender's first electric model went on sale, the solid-bodied Fender Esquire. It's no coincidence that at exactly the same time, rock & roll bands started to appear in the USA. This was the beginning of an intensely creative period of musical experimentation and diversity that would last for three decades. That doesn't mean that rock music stagnated after the 1970s—far from it—but by that time, the essential groundbreaking work was over and the blueprints of the genre had been established.

Rock music was an entirely American invention, created by fusing blues, country, and jazz. These earlier styles had been born from a broad range of influences that included the traditional music of South America, Africa, and European folk and classical music. Immigrants came to the United States from every corner of the globe and brought with them their own music and instruments. It's really no surprise that America dominated the popular music world of the twentieth century, and continues to dominate the twenty-first. Where else in the world could you have found a music scene shaped by so many cultural influences?

Rock & roll was not a regional music and so can't be traced to a particular part of the United States. This was because it was born

in the age of radio; the seed was spread from radio broadcasts beginning with DJ Alan Freed in the early 1950s. Freed played a mix of rhythm & blues and country music to a multicultural audience from a radio station in Cleveland, Ohio.

Many of the early rock & roll bands were basically jump-jive bands and had more to do with jazz than rock. So the most significant of all the early rock & roll performers was, without question, Elvis Presley. He set the world on fire with his music. It seems unbelievable now, but early television performances were censored and showed him only from the waist up—his famous gyrating moves were considered too sexual for television audiences. Elvis's guitarist throughout the 1950s was Scotty Moore, who was pivotal in creating the early rock guitar style. Another important musician was Chuck Berry. Although he was heavily influenced by the first electric blues guitarist, T-Bone Walker, Berry established the heavy riffing style and "straight eighths" groove of this exciting new music.

After its birth in the 1950s, rock & roll entered its most diverse period of growth, experimentation, and development.

The Fender Esquire remained popular for decades. It was played by guitarists such as Paul McCartney, Dave Gilmour, Bruce Springsteen, and—as here—Pink Floyd's Syd Barrett.

HISTORY OF ROCK

The 1960s was the decade that, for the only period in the history of popular music, saw America briefly unseated from its position of musical power and influence. The "British invasion" began with The Beatles and ended with Led Zeppelin, such was the fast-changing scene in this decade. The Beatles were the first group based outside the States to have an impact on American popular music and culture. They were also pioneers of the new rock sound. Gone were the last remnants of country, jazz, and blues. Rock now was new and hip! While The Beatles created a brand new sound, another

Alan Freed—the father of rock & roll. Freed popularized the genre and coined its name.

movement was simultaneously refocusing the world on a more traditional style: The British blues boom. Drawing heavily on the music of the African-American blues musicians, the British pioneers blended the heavy riffing of artists such as Howlin' Wolf, Bo Diddley, and Muddy Waters with the virtuoso soloing style of players like BB King, Freddie King, and Buddy Guy. At the forefront of this movement was Eric Clapton. The guitar god was born. From his work with John Mayall's Bluesbreakers, Cream, Blind Faith, and Derek And The Dominoes, plus his huge solo career, Clapton is probably the most famous guitarist in the world. And there's no doubt that in everything from tone to phrasing, riffs, licks, and even effects, Clapton is one of the most important rock guitarists. His virtuosity was exceeded by only one man: Jimi Hendrix. Hendrix had already been playing the American R & B circuit for several years, supporting famous artists from The Isley Brothers to Little Richard. After a subsequent attempt to go solo flopped, Animals bassist-turned-manager Chas Chandler flew him over to London's burgeoning rock scene, and the rest is history. Hendrix raised the bar and set new standards for the guitar hero status. He was the complete package: musician, songwriter, showman, and fashion icon. His incredible talents towered over those who followed in his wake, and his influence can still be heard in rock music today.

As the decade progressed, those early pioneers The Beatles remained a powerful defining force in rock music. Their 1967 album *Sgt. Pepper's Lonely Hearts Club Band* was a seminal release in rock history: it was the first concept album and laid the foundations for not just prog rock, but for the rock-focused album market that was to thrive for the next two decades. Rock music, overnight, became a serious art form. In the wake of this important transition, prog rock pioneers Pink Floyd, Yes, and Genesis were formed. Simultaneously, two of the most important bands in rock's history were taking their first tentative steps: Led Zeppelin and Black Sabbath. Zeppelin were formed in 1968 out of the ashes of The Yardbirds by guitarist Jimmy Page. Page was also a successful session musician and recruited fellow session keyboardist/bassist John Paul Jones along with unknown drummer John Bonham and vocalist Robert Plant to complete the line-up. There is perhaps no other group that has had such a profound and lasting influence on rock music. By coincidence, Black Sabbath was also formed in the same year. The quartet of unknown English musicians, fronted by vocalist Ozzy Osbourne and guitarist Tony Iommi, defined the heavy metal sound. Iommi's drop-tuned riffs continue to influence guitarists to this day.

The 1970s began with a rude awakening. The hippie movement was over. Jimi Hendrix, Brian Jones, Janis Joplin, and Jim Morrison were all dead (and had all died aged just 27). The harsh reality that the revolution hadn't happened was kicking in. But rock moved on, and the early 1970s was a hugely creative time for music. By the end of the decade it had mutated into a multitude of subgenres: heavy metal, prog rock, blues rock, country rock, neo-classical rock, jazz rock, stadium rock... the list just kept growing. Of course the true pioneers in any style don't set out with the intention of creating a brand new genre—they just want to make the best music they can. It's the music journalists and critics who come up with the labels, after the event. By the end of the decade American and British rock were drifting apart. The UK was regressing, musically speaking, as punk and new wave spread across the land. In the States punk never really enjoyed success outside the clubs of New York. Rock was still king, and guitarists like Eddie Van Halen were taking rock guitar to a new level of virtuosity with their two-handed tapping techniques.

In the early 1980s, Britain pioneered the rebirth of heavy rock with "new wave" heavy metal bands such as Iron Maiden, Def Leppard, Motörhead, and Judas Priest updating the sound with deeper, faster riffs. American bands such as Metallica, Slayer, Megadeth, and Anthrax picked up the mantle—and took things further with the fast and furious new sound of thrash metal.

During the late 1980s, the alternative rock movement was gaining momentum on both sides of the Atlantic. As the antidote to the overblown and overindulgent fast solos of the new metal styles, alternative rock championed simple riffs and catchy melodies—a return to the pop sound of the early 1960s. Bands such as REM, The Smiths, and The Cure were early pioneers of the style that enjoyed a sustained success throughout the 1980s and 1990s.

The "back to basics" philosophy of the early alternative rock bands had set the seeds for another new sound. The 1990s kicked off with grunge rock (Nirvana, Pearl Jam, and Soundgarden) in America, and swiftly followed with the Britpop backlash in the UK (Oasis, Pulp, and Blur). Both movements represented a return to a simplistic, song-based style with strong post-punk leanings. Long guitar solos were definitely out!

Rock music in the new millennium has continued to thrive. Perhaps not quite so widely listened to, or held in such high esteem as it once was, but it is alive and kicking nonetheless. This umbrella term covers such a wide range of subgenres that it is really no longer acceptable to describe a music as simply "rock"; further classification is needed before it can have any meaning. Today, people refer to music recorded in rock's heyday of the 1960s and 1970s as classic rock. The contemporary obsession with rock history is not just about nostalgia; classic rock has found a new, younger audience of people who weren't even born the first time round!

There are two clear reasons why this music was so good and has never been equalled since: firstly, the competition—there were far more bands around, so the standard was much higher as bands strove to beat their rivals' latest album; and secondly, business—the musicians were still in charge of the music and record companies were still investing in long-term careers. Plus live music reverberated throughout every town in the land, most nights of the week, so we didn't need TV shows to invent new talent. Check out some essential classic rock tracks and see how they grab you—the sheer power and collective skill of the early Led Zeppelin recordings; the hypnotic sound of Black Sabbath letting rip; or Dave Gilmour's soaring solos (with a tone to die for) on

Artists such as the Rolling Stones have had their careers revitalized, decades after they burst onto the scene, by the renewed interest in classic rock from a younger generation.

those classic 1970s Pink Floyd albums. These moments are unlikely to be created again, because time—and music—have moved on. That doesn't mean that music won't ever be good again, just different. So use this book to gain an insight into the playing style of the most important players in rock's history, absorb their styles, and go create your own!

THE CAGED SYSTEM

The CAGED system is a beautifully conceived philosophy that rationalizes the guitar's bewildering fretboard layout. Once you start using it you'll wonder how anyone could play effectively without it. Every pro uses this system, which organizes the fretboard into five distinct zones. The pattern used for each zone remains constant in every key (but moves to a different fret), and can be applied to chord shapes, arpeggios, scale patterns, and riffs or licks. If you can play it, then it can be CAGED! And by practicing new material in each of the five shapes, transposing it to other keys becomes a breeze.

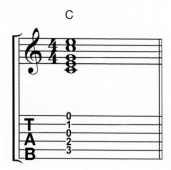

CAGED is an acronym for those five open major chord shapes that every fledgling guitarist takes their first steps with. And in case you haven't played them for a while, here's a reminder (see top right):

To achieve the CAGED mapping system, these five shapes need to be transposed to become tonic chords in the same key (i.e. all C major chords). Before you can relocate them, the shapes need to be converted to moveable forms by barring with your first finger where the open strings occur. Finally they are placed end to end along the fretboard, covering the entire neck in C chords (bottom right):

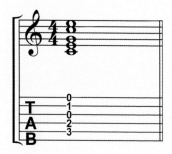

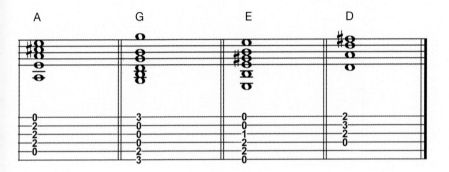

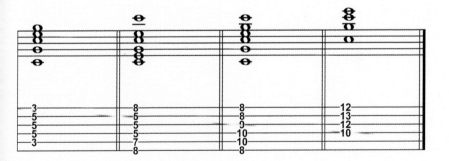

THE CAGED SYSTEM

Because all Shape 1 patterns (chords/arpeggios/scales) are derived from the open E shape, it actually makes more sense to reorganize the chords as EDCAG. This makes for a more logical system that begins with Shape One and ascends to Shape Five. Here the system is re-jigged to show all five shapes as F major chords, starting with a Shape One barre chord in its lowest position.

The CAGED system is used throughout this book, both in the licks and scales and in the chops builder sections. To avoid confusion, reference to the original open chord shape has been dropped in preference to an EDCAG numerical reference (e.g. Shape 1, Shape 4, etc). This is common practice in educational establishments and guitar publications worldwide.

Shape One

Shape Two Shape Three Shape Four Shape Five

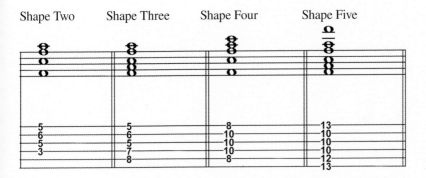

READING TAB

TAB is short for tablature, a simplified system of notation that's widely used for guitar. Many people wrongly assume that this is a modern system born out of the Internet, but it actually dates back to the Renaissance (c.1400–1600) when it was used to notate music for the lute. Today it's used in music publications worldwide, and is the most common form of guitar notation. TAB uses six lines, each one symbolizing one of the guitar's six strings. Numbers are written on the lines to indicate the frets played. It's as simple as that.

In example 1 you can see how the six open strings of the guitar are represented in TAB form (remember the sixth string is the lowest!).

Hammer-ons and pull-offs are indicated by a bracket between the two notes (example 2). Pick the first note only—the second pitch is created by firmly fretting the higher note (hammer on) or flicking your fretting finger sideways as you release it (pull off).

Slides are indicated by a straight line drawn between the two pitches (example 3). Pick only the first note and slide up (or down) the fretboard to the second note without removing your finger from the string.

Ex1 The open strings

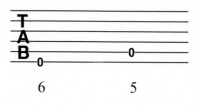

Ex2 Hammer-ons and pull-offs

Ex3 Slides

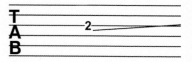

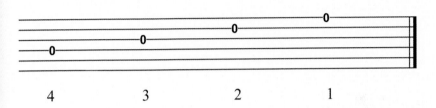

4   3   2   1

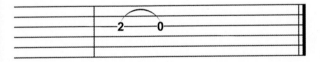

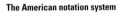

The American notation system

Traditional note names
have been shunned in favor
of the American system
throughout this book. That's
because it's easier to
understand: a whole note
lasts a full bar, and there
are four quarter notes in a
regular bar of 4/4.

The equivalent "old school"
names are given below for
reference:
Whole note = Semibreve
Half note = Minim
Quarter note = Crotchet
Eighth note = Quaver
Sixteenth note = Semiquaver

READING TAB

String bends (example 4) are achieved by fretting the first note, and then bending up to the virtual pitch indicated by the symbol above the bend arrow (see legend right). Bend and release simply involves a release back to the original pitch (in brackets). A pre-bend release involves bending the string to the fret indicated, picking the note, and then releasing it to its normal pitch as shown in brackets.

Vibrato (example 5) is always indicated by a single wavy line above a note. Some blues players (most notably BB King and Eric Clapton) execute vibrato with their thumb off the neck to intensify the effect. This will be mentioned in the text when it is required.

Two-Handed Tapping (example 6) is used to create impressive legato passages. Pitches are created by tapping the first finger of your picking hand on the fretboard of the guitar at the fret indicated in the TAB. The 'T' indicates which notes should be tapped. Following pitches are generated by pulling off the finger to the fretted note, which is usually followed by a hammer-on as in the example below.

Trills (example 7) are created by a brisk oscillation with a note a whole step or half step above. These are not written rhythmically but indicated as shown. Pick only the first note and use consecutive hammer-ons and pull-offs to create the trill effect.

Ex4 String Bends

1) whole step bend

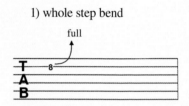

Ex5 Vibrato

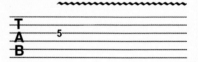

Ex7 Trills

1) whole step trill

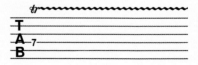

Bending Legend

¼ = quarter tone (less than one fret) bend

½ = half step (one fret) bend

Full = whole step (two frets) bend

1½ = one and a half step (three frets) bend

2 = two whole steps (four frets) bend

2) half step bend & release   3) whole step pre-bend release

Ex6 Two-Handed Tapping

2) half step trill

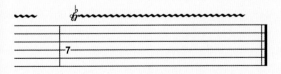

THE ROMAN NUMERAL SYSTEM

Professional musicians don't just think of chords as A7, G minor, or E. They think of the root notes in relation to the tonic of the key they are playing in. This system makes for easy transposition, allowing a chord sequence to be played in any key, instantly. It also means that familiar chord sequences are instantly recognizable (e.g. turnarounds, cadences, or entire progressions like a 12-bar blues)—particularly useful when you're faced with the prospect of improvising. The pro can identify chord sequences just by listening. This doesn't require perfect pitch (which is not possessed by the majority of musicians), just a highly developed ear. It's a great tool to possess, and can be learned over time just like any other skill. Next time you hear a tune on the radio, concentrate on the bass line. Once you can identify the root movement

Fig1 Basic 12-bar blues

of a chord progression, filling in the details (whether the chord is major, minor, or a dominant seventh) should be easy.

When notating a chord sequence in this way, Roman numerals are always used. This is an established harmonic convention, and not just a feature of this book. The 12-bar blues would be described as a I, IV, V sequence because it contains chords built on the tonic (I), the perfect fourth (IV), and the perfect fifth (V). It's exactly the same as describing the intervals of a scale.

For instance, below, the minor pentatonic is first described as a scale formula (indicating the intervals of the scale), and then in Roman numerals (describing a minor pentatonic chord sequence). Accidentals are necessary in both scenarios:

Minor Pentatonic:
   1 – b3 – 4 – 5 – b7
Minor Pentatonic Chord Progression:
   I – bIII – IV – V – bVII

THE ROMAN NUMERAL SYSTEM

Here's how the Roman numeral system relates to the chords of a basic 12-bar blues—see figure 1 on the previous page. The chord symbols are in the key of C, but the Roman numerals could be applied to any key. Because it's understood that all the chords in the progression are dominant sevenths, there's no need to add a "7" after each number.

More complex "changes" (a term musicians use to describe chord progressions) could add a quick change in bar 2, a diminished chord in bar 6, and a "turnaround" in bars 11 and 12. This is how a more complex chord sequence would be written with chord symbols (again in C major) and Roman numerals. Notice that non-diatonic chords (i.e. containing notes outside of the key) are always qualified when they occur (hence F#° is written as #IV° and A7 as VI7)—see figure 2.

Every lick in this book has been categorized by its relationship to a particular section of the basic or complex blues progression. Many of the chapters are based entirely on "Chord IV" or "Chord V" licks in a particular subgenre or player's style. This will help you to get the most out of every lick. Played in a harmonic vacuum, the coolest lick in the world would be totally meaningless.

Fig2 Complex 12-bar blues

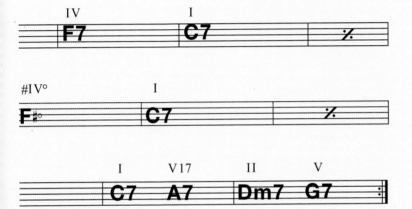

KILLER LICKS

RIFF NO. 1:

SCOTTY MOORE OPEN E STYLE

As Elvis Presley's original guitarist, Scotty Moore was an important figure in the evolution of rock guitar technique. He was fluent in jazz and country music and borrowed elements of both styles to create his trademark technique. Early rock & roll tunes were usually based on the 12-bar blues form; so this distinctive, jangly riff would be paired with similarly picked open A7 and B7 chords to provide a full song accompaniment.

"That's All Right"–Elvis Presley's first single (1954)

WATCH OUT FOR

HOLD DOWN THE OPEN E CHORD THROUGHOUT. LIFT OFF YOUR FIRST FINGER TO PLAY THE OPEN THIRD STRING AND ADD THE C# ON THE SECOND STRING WITH YOUR FOURTH FINGER.

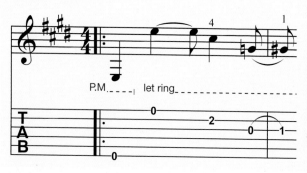

ROCK & ROLL RIFFS

RIFF REGISTER

Function: Tonic (I) chord riff in a 50s rock & roll 12-bar.

Technique: Finger-style or pick-style. When playing finger-style a root and fifth bass line can be added with the thumb.

EDCAG position: Shape 1 E major chord.

Harmonic content: Tonic major chord with added sixth (C#) and chromatic approach to major third (G–G#).

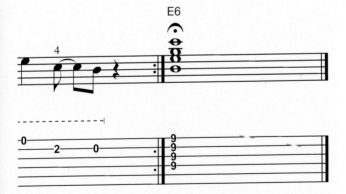

RIFF NO. 2:

BOOGIE-WOOGIE-STYLE RIFF

1950s rock & roll guitarists were true pioneers—they were creating a brand new style of music with no guidelines to help them. Riffs and licks were often borrowed from earlier styles of music, but sounded fresh and exciting in a new, youthful musical setting. This example is typical of early rock & roll riffs, and would have been inspired by the boogie-woogie piano style of the late 1930s and early 1940s.

Rock & roll style was youthful, daring, and innovative

WATCH OUT FOR

MUTING THE SECOND STRING. USE YOUR FIRST FINGER TO BARRE THE NOTES ON THE MIDDLE STRINGS; BY BENDING YOUR FINGER SLIGHTLY AT THE FIRST JOINT, YOU CAN EASILY DAMP THE SECOND STRING.

$\quartnote$ = 200 swing

ROCK & ROLL RIFFS

RIFF REGISTER

Function: Tonic (I) riff in a 12-bar rock & roll song. Can be started on the fourth string for the D (IV) or down to the sixth for E (V) in this key.

Technique: Use alternate eighth-note picking throughout. Can be played finger-style for a tighter sound.

EDCAG position: Shape 4 open A power chord using third and fourth fingers to add extra notes on the fifth and fourth strings.

Harmonic content: Open power chord shape with added sixth and minor seventh. The major third (C#) is only stated as a low note on the fifth string.

RIFF NO. 3:
SCOTTY MOORE OPEN A-STYLE

Evidence of Scotty Moore's country music background can be heard in many of his earliest accompaniments. Unlike the previous riff, this example would be used in conjunction with finger-picked open chords—it's not designed to be moved onto the other strings. The rising bass line at the end of the second bar includes the major seventh (G#), which pulls back to the tonic (A) and adds a country flavor.

Scotty Moore playing
Gibson L-5 CES, 1955

WATCH OUT FOR
PLAY THE A7 FRAGMENT ON THE FIFTH FRET BY BARRING ACROSS THE STRINGS WITH YOUR FIRST FINGER. THE MAJOR THIRD (C#) IS ADDED BY HAMMERING ON YOUR SECOND FINGER.

$\quad$ = 190 swing

A7

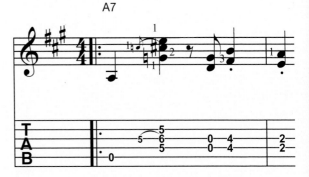

ROCK & ROLL RIFFS

RIFF REGISTER

Function: Two-bar open A7 riff used only on the tonic (I) chord.

Technique: Can be played finger-style or pick-style. Palm muting is essential for the low notes with both techniques.

EDCAG position: Shape 1 A7 chord fragment moving to open A5 chord.

Harmonic content: A7 vamp that adds the major sixth (F#) and ninth (B) at the end of the first bar and chromatic approach to root note (major seventh) before repeating.

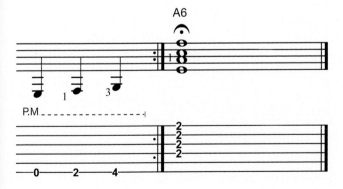

RIFF NO. 4:

DOUBLE STOPS-STYLE RIFF

Double stops are achieved by playing two notes simultaneously. They can be mixed with arpeggios to create driving, syncopated riffs—perfect as a verse accompaniment. In this example the double stop is a major third, which is played a half step lower before being repeated on the off beat. Double stops can consist of any interval, but thirds, fourths, and sixths are the most common.

Steve Cropper playing
in Copenhagen with
Booker T & The MGs

WATCH OUT FOR

HOLD DOWN THE SHAPE 3 CHORD IN THE SECOND BAR, SWEEPING DOWN WITH YOUR PICK AS INDICATED WHEN PLAYING THE GRACE NOTES. THE HIGH D IS ADDED WITH YOUR FOURTH FINGER (WITHOUT RELEASING THE CHORD SHAPE).

ROCK & ROLL RIFFS

RIFF REGISTER

Function: Two-bar arpeggio-based riff used as a repeated figure in a verse section.

Technique: Works best when played with a pick. Sweep picking (a single down or up stroke dragged across the strings) is used for the rake in the second bar.

EDCAG position: Shape 3 G major triad on the top four strings.

Harmonic content: The plain sounding major arpeggio is "spiced up" with a chromatic approach (i.e., the double stop is played a half step lower before being repeated) in the first bar.

let ring _ |

LICK NO. 1:
COUNTRY-STYLE CHROMATIC LICK

In early rock & roll recordings, the solos were often based around arpeggios (i.e., using the notes of a chord), just as they would have been in country and jazz. This arpeggio-based lick also incorporates chromatic dissonance (simultaneously sounding a fretted note against an open string that's a half step higher), a technique borrowed from country music. Dissonance creates excitement in music—as long as it's resolved!

Bill Haley in concert

ROCK & ROLL LICKS

RIFF REGISTER

Function: Tonic chord lick based on the arpeggio (chord notes) of E major. Works well as an opening or concluding lick since it resolves on the root note.

Technique: Early rock & roll was either fast (up-tempo swing) or slow (12/8 ballad). When fast, use strict alternate eighth-note picking!

EDCAG position: Shape 1 E major arpeggio using open strings.

Harmonic content: E major arpeggio notes with added chromatic approach notes (i.e., play the note one fret lower before playing the note you want!).

WATCH OUT FOR

TRY TO GET THE PAIRS OF NOTES ON THE FIRST TWO BEATS OF THE SECOND BAR TO RING INTO EACH OTHER, BY KEEPING YOUR THIRD FINGER FRETTED WHILE YOU PICK THE OPEN STRING ABOVE IN EACH CASE.

LICK NO. 2:
OPEN BLUES SCALE LICK

Rock & roll guitarists borrowed much from the blues—so quarter tone bends and the blues scale (the minor pentatonic with a b5 passing note) became *de rigueur*. The minor third (G) in this lick is bent slightly sharp to make the scale "fit" over the E7 chord. The flattened fifth is sounded directly against the chord in the second bar but should be played staccato, leaving the listener waiting for the resolution provided by the next note.

Big Bill Broonzy in the 1940s

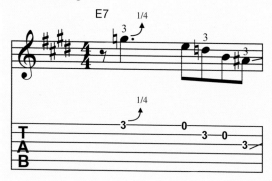

RIFF REGISTER

Function: Blues scale-based lick played over the tonic chord. Works well in a solo and because it's short, can also be used as a fill between vocal phrases.

Technique: Played with a pick using alternate eighth-note picking. An up-pick is an option, but it will sound stronger if you use a down-pick.

EDCAG position: Shape 1 E blues scale.

Harmonic content: Blues scale tensions are forced over a dominant seventh chord to create tension, released by resolving on to a sustained root note.

LICK NO. 3:
SYNCOPATION WITH UNISON SLIDES

Unison slides are achieved by sliding a lower note to the same pitch as a higher string. They sound good because of the way the notes are accented, to create syncopation. This lick masks beat one in bars two and four by emphasizing the fourth beat of the previous bar. Rhythm is vital in rock & roll, where the emphasis of the backbeat (beats 2 and 4) is more pronounced than in other styles.

T-Bone Walker
performing in
London, 1967

RIFF REGISTER

Function: Strong solo opener or intro lick. The last note would also work when resolving onto chord IV (A7) in a 12-bar style rock & roll solo.

Technique: Use alternate picking throughout. Make sure you're playing a strong down-pick on the fourth beat of the first bar and third beat of the second.

EDCAG position: Shape 2 moving to shape 1 E blues scale.

Harmonic content: E blues scale forces minor thirds and sevenths over a tonic major chord. Diminished fifth used as passing note in the second bar.

WATCH OUT FOR
GETTING THAT TRICKY SYNCOPATED RHYTHM RIGHT. TRY CLAPPING THROUGH THE FIRST TWO BARS BEFORE YOU PLAY THEM.

LICK NO. 4:
BANJO ROLL-STYLE

Tunes played at slower 12/8 tempos were a rock & roll mainstay, as they provided relief from up-tempo swing grooves for musicians and dancers alike. Banjo rolls (repeatedly sounding fretted notes against open strings) had long been a feature of country music, and country guitarists had adapted the banjo roll for guitar. Rock & roll guitarists like Chet Atkins, keen to add flashy licks to their solos, were quick to adopt the technique.

Chet Atkins in 1965

WATCH OUT FOR

KEEPING PICKING ALTERNATE. YOU SHOULD START BEATS 1 AND 3 WITH A DOWN-PICK IN EVERY BAR IF YOU'RE DOING IT RIGHT. START SLOWLY, SETTING YOUR METRONOME TO GIVE AN EIGHTH-NOTE PULSE.

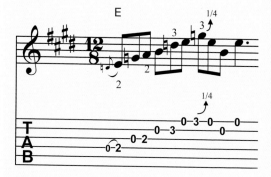

ROCK & ROLL LICKS

RIFF REGISTER

Function: Tonic blues scale lick ideal for creating a climatic ending phrase to a solo or song.

Technique: It will feel strange at first (because you'll be starting beats two and four with an up-pick), but stick to alternate eighth-note picking to achieve maximum fluency.

EDCAG position: Shape 1 E blues scale.

Harmonic content: E minor pentatonic. High minor third bent up a quarter-tone to create a "blue note" over E major chord.

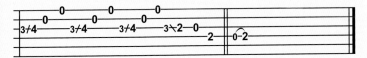

RIFF NO. 1:
STRAIGHT RIFF VS SWING GROOVE

During the early days of rock & roll, the up-tempo swing grooves of jazz and jump jive formed the basis of the rhythm section's accompaniment. Guitarists, on the other hand, were creating a new sound by playing straight eighth riffs against this underlying swing groove. Many of Chuck Berry's classic songs were formed around this unusual mix of styles.

Chuck Berry in concert, 1973

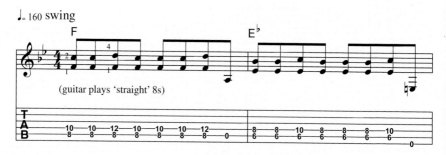

(guitar plays 'straight' 8s)

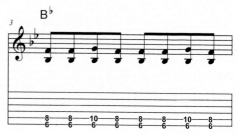

RIFF REGISTER

Function: Straight eighths riff that functions over bars 9 to 12 in a 12-bar blues-based rock & roll form.

EDCAG position: Shape 4 major chord-based riff, moving to shape 1 in the third bar.

Technique: Although this is an up-tempo eighth-note riff, a more even, driving groove can be achieved by using down-picks throughout.

Harmonic content: Ambiguous "power chord" voicings contain no thirds, but oscillate the perfect fifth and sixth above the root note to create a driving riff.

WATCH OUT FOR

PLAYING A REGULAR SHUFFLE GROOVE. PRACTICE PLAYING THIS RIFF WITH BOTH A STRAIGHT AND SHUFFLE FEEL SO THAT YOU CAN DIFFERENTIATE BETWEEN THE TWO.

LICK NO. 2:
DOUBLE-STOP LICK USING "SIXTHS"

Major and minor sixths had long been a feature of country guitarists' solos and soon became a part of rock & roll vocabulary. The early rock & roll tunes were also often played in guitar-unfriendly flat keys because these were the common keys of the day (favored by horn players in jazz); guitar players had yet to assert their preference for sharp keys (to facilitate the use of open strings and chords).

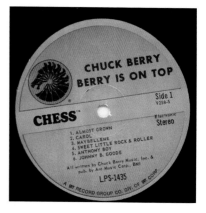

Album artwork for
Chuck Berry's *Berry is
on Top* (1959)

WATCH OUT FOR

DAMPING THE SURROUNDING STRINGS WHEN YOU'RE PLAYING THE SIXTHS IN THE SECOND BAR. BY ANGLING YOUR SECOND FINGER SLIGHTLY, YOU WILL BE ABLE TO MUTE THE FOURTH AND SECOND STRINGS SIMULTANEOUSLY.

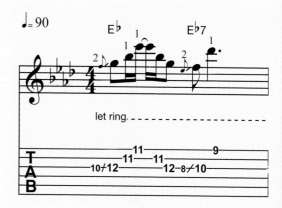

THE CHUCK BERRY-STYLE

RIFF REGISTER

Function: Lick over bars 9 and 10 of a 12-bar rock & roll sequence.

Technique: Alternate picking should be used on staggered sixths (i.e., when the notes are not played simultaneously), picking up on the higher note. Use a single downstroke to play the double-stop sixths at the end of the second bar.

EDCAG position: Shape 1 Eb major triad. Descending sixths in the second bar start in shape 2 and conclude in shape 1.

Harmonic content: The minor sixth played against the Eb7 chord in the first bar, creates dominant ninth color tones over the chord.

LICK NO. 3:
SYNCOPATED DOUBLE-STOP LICK

This Chuck Berry-style lick is based on a simple root and major third double stop. Obviously these notes would sound uninspiring either just sustained against the chord, or played dead on the beat. By using syncopation (the emphasis of weak beats) throughout the first and third bars, these double stops are transformed into a cool, driving lick.

Chuck Berry in concert, 1973

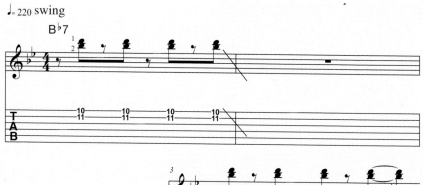

RIFF REGISTER

Function: Works well as either a mid-solo or opening lick over the tonic chord. Could also be used as an ending lick.

Technique: Use alternate picking throughout to create a smooth, swinging, rhythmic delivery.

EDCAG position: Shape 2 Bb major chord shape (using only the highest two notes).

Harmonic content: Major and minor third voiced high over a tonic dominant seventh chord (also works well over the tonic major since the minor seventh is not included).

WATCH OUT FOR

BARRING THE CONCLUDING DOUBLE STOPS WITH ONE FINGER AS INDICATED IN THE FOURTH BAR. USING A FINGER FOR EACH NOTE OF THE DOUBLE STOP WILL SIMPLY SLOW YOU DOWN AT THIS FAST TEMPO.

RIFF NO. 4:
BLUES-FLAVORED DOUBLE-STOP RIFF

Forcing minor thirds over major chords had been a feature of blues solos and riffs for decades by the time rock & roll was born. Chuck Berry incorporated the idea into his style, mixing the "blue" thirds with riffs and chords. Using a quarter-tone bend to tweak the minor third (Bb) while sounding it against the perfect fifth (D) above creates a distinctive-sounding double stop—"just like a ringin' a bell," as Berry puts it in "Johnny B. Goode."

Gibson ES335 guitar

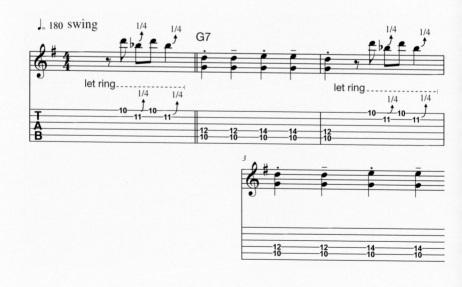

THE CHUCK BERRY-STYLE

RIFF REGISTER

Function: Tonic riff based on a high double-stop lick alternated with a simple power chord shape. Ideal for intros or for use between verses.

Technique: The high lick should be played using alternate picking, starting with an up-pick with the first note (high D).

EDCAG position: Shape 4 minor pentatonic lick and power chord.

Harmonic content: The minor third is bent up a quarter-tone and sounded with the perfect fifth. This, used in conjunction with the power chord riff, creates a harmonically ambiguous accompaniment—still an important feature of rock music.

WATCH OUT FOR

BECAUSE THIS RIFF HINTS AT A COUNTRY-STYLE DOUBLE-TIME CUT GROOVE, THE G7 RIFF IS WRITTEN AS QUARTER NOTES. PLAY THE NOTES ALTERNATELY STACCATO AND LEGATO AS INDICATED, OR YOUR RIFF WILL NOT SWING.

LICK NO. 1:
THE SOLO OPENER

One of the most important elements of
any solo is the lick you start with. A
cool opening phrase grabs the listener's
attention and sets you off on the right
footing for the rest of the solo. There's
nothing worse than trying to recover from
a hapless flurry of notes, so practice a
classy moveable opening lick—it can be
shifted to any key you want simply by
moving the pattern up or down the neck.

A Wurlitzer—the
iconic jukebox of
the rock & roll era

M O V E A B L E   R O C K   &   R O L L   L I C K S

RIFF REGISTER

Function: Two-bar lick that's perfect as a solo opener.

Technique: Slurred lick that relies on a strong pull-off technique. Flick your finger sideways as you release it from the string for best results.

EDCAG position: Shape 1 dorian mode/blues scale.

Harmonic content: The upper notes of E dorian mode superimpose the minor third over the tonic major chord. It also adds the major sixth and ninth color tones, which occur as passing notes in the opening bar.

WATCH OUT FOR

BARRING YOUR FIRST FINGER ACROSS THE TWELFTH FRET FOR THE DOUBLE PULL-OFFS ON THE HIGHEST STRINGS. AT THIS TEMPO YOU DON'T NEED TO WORRY ABOUT DAMPING A STRING YOU'RE NOT PLAYING.

LICK NO. 2:
THE SONG OPENER

In the blues, an instrumental introduction often featured an unaccompanied lick from the guitarist over the first four bars of a 12-bar sequence; the band would then enter in the fifth bar (on the IV chord) and the guitar solo would continue. Many rock & roll tunes borrowed this idea, most famously Chuck Berry's "Roll Over Beethoven" and "Johnny B. Goode."

Chuck Berry live onstage in Finsbury Park, London, 1966

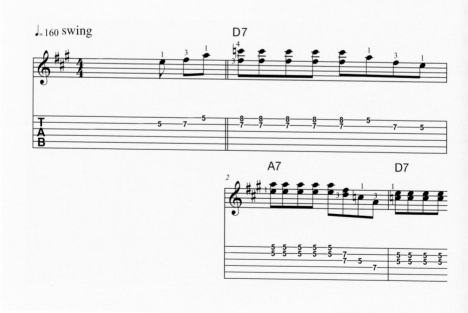

M O V E A B L E R O C K & R O L L L I C K S

RIFF REGISTER

Function: Unaccompanied intro lick based on the first four bars of a 12-bar sequence. Although this would normally consist of four bars of the tonic, this example alternates between chord IV and I.

Technique: Play the double stops with down-picks to emphasize the "straight eighths" phrasing.

EDCAG position: Shape 4 D mixolydian and shape 1 A mixolydian.

Harmonic content: The F# and C are the major third and minor seventh of the D7 chord. Play as a double stop to form a flattened fifth interval, creating anticipation before the band enter in the fifth bar.

WATCH OUT FOR

THE TEMPORARY SHIFT OUT OF POSITION
AT THE END OF THE THIRD BAR—USE THE
FINGERING INDICATED AND PRACTICE SLOWLY
BEFORE YOU ATTEMPT THE LICK AT TEMPO.

A7

LICK NO. 3:

THE ENDING PHRASE

To end a song, the guitarist traditionally plays a two-bar lick with the rhythm section also phrasing the push into the last chord on the fourth beat. Ending licks are important—whether you're signing off a solo or ending a whole tune, this is the lick people will remember. Don't forget you can move this lick to the key you want by moving the pattern up or down the neck.

Everything in the 1950s—not just guitar-playing—was big and flashy

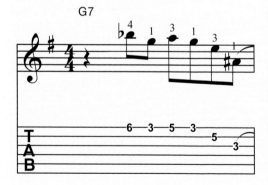

RIFF REGISTER

Function: Works as either a solo ending or song ending based on the tonic chord.

Technique: Use alternate picking throughout to create a smooth, swinging, rhythmic delivery.

EDCAG position: Shape 2 Bb major chord shape (using only the highest two notes).

Harmonic content: Major and minor third voiced high over a tonic dominant seventh chord (also works well over the tonic major since the minor seventh is not included).

LICK NO. 4:
ALTERNATING BETWEEN STRAIGHT AND SWING

Playing straight eighth phrases over a swing groove is a common feature of jazz improvisation (listen to anything by the great guitarist Pat Martino) but it also sounds cool in rock & roll. Alternating between straight and swing eighths over a swing groove will add a new dimension to your solos. This lick opens with a series of driving double stops played with a straight feel. The final bar is played with a swing feel to heighten the conclusion.

Pat Martino, 1990

MOVEABLE ROCK & ROLL LICKS

RIFF REGISTER

Function: Four-bar tonic lick that works equally well over major or dominant seventh chords.

Technique: The straight feel of the double stops can be heightened by using down-picks in the first three bars. Switch to alternate picking in the final bar.

EDCAG position: Shape 1 E major arpeggio-based lick concluding in shape 1 E mixolydian (with added minor third).

Harmonic content: Chromatically approach each double stop, so each pair of arpeggio notes is emphasized. Minor third and major sixth are stated in the final bar, adding tension.

WATCH OUT FOR

SWITCHING FROM STRAIGHT TO SWING FEEL ON THE FLY. TO GAIN CONFIDENCE, PRACTICE PLAYING ALTERNATE BARS OF STRAIGHT AND SWING FEELS WITH A METRONOME.

RIFF NO. 1:

RICKENBACKER 12-STRING RIFF

Rickenbacker guitars were an integral part of The Beatles' sound. John Lennon bought his first Rickenbacker during the group's first tour of Germany in 1960. When Rickenbacker launched the 360 12-string in 1964, George Harrison received one of these pioneering instruments as a gift from the company's owner, and one of the iconic sounds of the decade was born.

George Harrison on the set of *A Hard Day's Night*, playing Rickenbacker 360/12 (1964)

WATCH OUT FOR

BECAUSE THE EM CHORD IS PICKED AND NOT STRUMMED, THERE'S NO NEED TO FRET THE LOWER NOTE ON THE FIFTH STRING.

RIFF REGISTER

Function: Simple two-bar riff that sounds much bigger than the sum of its parts when played on a 12-string electric.

Technique: Arpeggio pattern that sounds best when played with alternate eighth-note picking.

EDCAG position: Shape 1 open E minor chord.

Harmonic content: E minor arpeggio with major second and ninth added as passing notes. The riff concludes on the minor seventh to create a "pull" back to the tonic note on the repeat.

Asus2

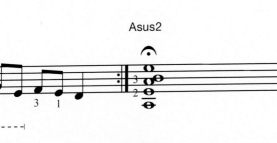

RIFF NO. 2:
DOUBLE-TRACKED RIFF

The Beatles stunned the world in 1967 with the release of *Sgt. Pepper's Lonely Hearts Club Band*, an album which changed the way popular music was recorded. Before this point, most artists cut their tracks live; what the band played was what you heard. *Sgt. Pepper's* showed that a much bigger sound could be created when extra tracks were overdubbed and instruments were multi-tracked.

Hand-painted bass drum skin, seen on the cover of *Sgt. Pepper's Lonely Hearts Club Band*

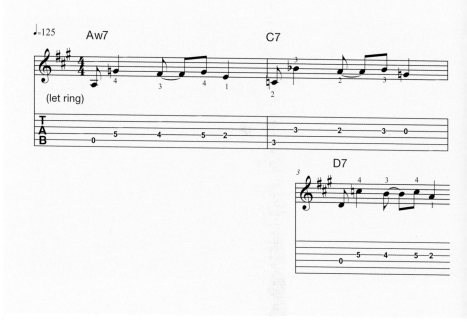

RIFF REGISTER

Function: One-bar riff that's transposed through a four-bar sequence to create an instrumental interlude.

Technique: Arpeggio patterns picked out of chord shapes using alternate eighth-note picking.

EDCAG position: Shape 4 dominant seventh chord shape.

Harmonic content: Harmonically ambiguous dominant seventh arpeggio riff (the major third is not played) with a major sixth added from mixolydian mode.

WATCH OUT FOR

ALTHOUGH IT'S NOT POSSIBLE TO ALLOW ALL THE NOTES TO RING ON, ALLOW THE LOWEST NOTE OF EACH CHORD TO RING THROUGHOUT EACH BAR. THIS CREATES A BIGGER, MORE JANGLY SOUND.

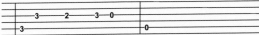

RIFF NO. 3:
BARRE CHORD-BASED RIFF

The Fab Four were the first rock group to use guitar riffs prominently in their songs, often as an attention-grabbing intro. Many of their early riffs were based around dominant seventh barre chord shapes. By incorporating hammer-ons and adding extra notes with the fourth finger to the chord shape, they created a new sound that heralded the beginning of the electric guitar's dominance of popular music.

Paul McCartney and George Harrison performing in a London TV studio, 1964

RIFF REGISTER

Function: Main song riff that would typically be used as an intro and/or interlude section.

Technique: Alternate picking is essential to achieve a fluid, rhythmic delivery.

EDCAG position: Shape 1 dominant seventh chord-based riff.

Harmonic content: Perfect fourth and major ninth intervals are added to the V dominant chord (B7). The riff is played a whole step lower over chord IV (A7), creating a bluesy, rock & roll style riff.

WATCH OUT FOR

HOLDING DOWN THE FULL BARRE CHORD SHAPE WHILE ADDING THE EXTRA NOTES ON THE THIRD AND FOURTH STRINGS WITH YOUR FOURTH FINGER. THIS MAY TAKE PRACTICE, PARTICULARLY THE STRETCH FOR THE EXTRA NOTE ON THE FOURTH STRING.

RIFF NO. 4:
LOW OPEN E RIFF

By playing an open string riff in the key of E, a bigger sound is created because it enables the lowest note (E) of the guitar to be used. To add extra "weight," riffs like this example would be doubled in unison by the bass. When used as the basis for a chorus sequence it provides a driving, syncopated rhythm. The Beatles were originally a dance band, so strong grooves were essential for getting the audience on their feet!

Cover of The Beatles' first album, *Please Please Me* (1963)

BEATLES-STYLE RIFFS

RIFF REGISTER

Function: Two-bar riff used to drive a song's chorus with an infectious, danceable rhythm.

Technique: Use alternate eighth-note picking throughout (there are only two up-picks, at the end of the first bar and beginning of the second).

EDCAG position: Shape 1 E mixolydian-based riff.

Harmonic content: This mixolydian-based riff is harmonized by the chords D (bVII), A (IV), and E (I)—a pioneering non-diatonic chord sequence that is still used in rock songs to this day.

WATCH OUT FOR

PREVENTING THE LOW OPEN A FROM RINGING INTO THE REPEAT. GENTLY TOUCH THE STRING WITH ANY FRETTING-HAND FINGER JUST BEFORE YOU PICK THE LOW E.

RIFF NO. 1:

ROBIN TROWER-STYLE

It was not until he formed his Hendrixesque power trio in the 1970s that Robin Trower's formidable talents were fully appreciated. Like Hendrix, Trower used a Univibe pedal to add the swirling sound that was characteristic of late 1960s and early 1970s blues rock. The Univibe pedal was the predecessor of the chorus pedal and had a much more organic, analog sound. You can hear it clearly on this riff.

Robin Trower, 1970

WATCH OUT FOR

THE SWIFT SIXTEENTH-NOTE PULL-OFF FOLLOWED BY A SLIDE INTO THE FOURTH BEAT IN THE FIRST BAR. USE THE FINGERING INDICATED (PARTICULARLY FOR THE SLIDE ON THE FIFTH STRING).

RIFF REGISTER

Function: Dark and menacing vamp functioning as the main riff in a heavy blues song.

Technique: Pull-offs and slides feature in the first bar. Fast sixteenth-note alternate picking is needed in the second bar for the three consecutive notes on the fifth string.

EDCAG position: Shape 1 blues scale.

Harmonic content: In typical blues rock style, this riff has no chordal accompaniment and is harmonically ambiguous. Equally effective in both major and minor keys.

Asus2

RIFF NO. 2:

ZZ TOP FUNKY BLUES

During the early 1970s, bands like The Allman Brothers and ZZ Top were fusing funk grooves with heavy blues riffs to create exciting new sounds. This ZZ Top style riff is typical of the era. The drum groove, with an accented open hi-hat at the end of each bar that locks with the guitar, drives this bluesy riff along relentlessly. The riff is double tracked on the CD and panned hard right and left—just as it would be on a ZZ Top album.

Album artwork for
ZZ Top, *Tres Hombres*
(1973)

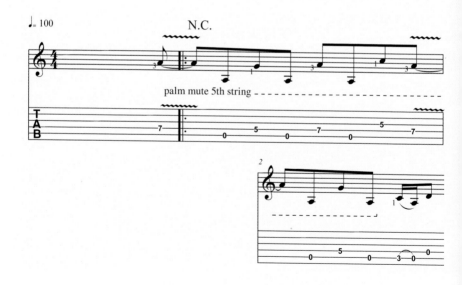

RIFF REGISTER

Function: Main riff of a hard, funky blues song. Also works well as a solo vamp.

Technique: Subtle palm muting is required to keep the bass notes (open A) sounding tight and prevent them from overpowering the riff's melody.

EDCAG position: Shape 1 minor pentatonic moving briefly to shape 4 at the end of the second bar.

Harmonic content: In true blues-rock style, the third (either major or minor) is avoided to enhance its harmonic ambiguity.

WATCH OUT FOR

ANTICIPATING THE FIRST NOTE OF EACH BAR ON THE OFF-BEAT OF THE PREVIOUS BAR. IF THIS NOTE IS PLAYED ON THE BEAT BY MISTAKE, THE RIFF WILL LOSE ALL ITS COOL, DRIVING SYNCOPATION.

RIFF NO. 3:
RORY GALLAGHER-STYLE

Rory Gallagher is one of the unsung guitar heroes of the 1970s. To those familiar with his work, he is a musician of integrity and quality. He shunned the lure of mainstream stardom when he famously turned down the opportunity to join The Rolling Stones in 1975. This riff is a tribute to his ability to turn three simple chords into a hypnotic, bluesy vamp that's guaranteed to get your feet tapping!

Rory Gallagher
performing in 1973

WATCH OUT FOR

THE QUICK CHANGE FROM THE G7 ARPEGGIO TO D5 IN THE SECOND BAR. BE SURE TO USE THE FINGERING AS INDICATED.

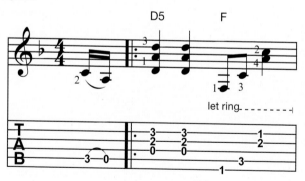

RIFF REGISTER

Function: Powerful three-chord riff that would typically be the basis of a blues-rock anthem.

Technique: Intricate picking and careful damping is required to avoid chord-based riffs from sounding messy, particularly when played with an overdriven sound.

EDCAG position: Shape 2 D power chord followed by shape 1 F major barre and open shape 5 G7 shape.

Harmonic content: Because the D chord is only played as a power chord, the underlying minor tonality of the riff is never established. Harmonic ambiguity is a desirable quality in all rock music.

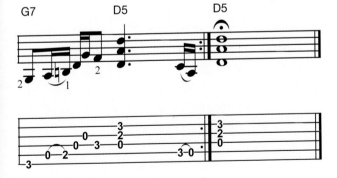

RIFF NO. 4:
FREE-STYLE

Free were one of the most successful British blues rock bands of the 1970s. During an era when flamboyant prog rock and androgynous glam rock were fashionable, Free stuck to their guns and played what they knew best: no-nonsense rock music with a blues influence. Guitarist Paul Kossoff died at the age of just 25, leaving behind a legacy of blues-rock albums that still sound as cool today as they did back in the early 1970s.

Album artwork for *The Free Story* (1974)

WATCH OUT FOR
AVOIDING INADVERTENTLY DAMPING THE OPEN THIRD STRING WHEN YOU'RE FRETTING THE SLIDES AT THE START OF THE SECOND BAR.

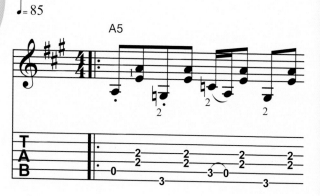

B L U E S - R O C K   R I F F S

RIFF REGISTER

Function: Percussive, driving, two-bar riff typically used as the main vamp in a blues-rock song.

Technique: Because of the repeating off-beat power chord, this riff can be played with either alternate picking or finger-style. The latter will heighten the syncopated quality of the off-beat chords.

EDCAG position: Shape 4 power chord-based riff with shape 2 D5 and shape 5 G5 power chords punctuating the end of the riff.

Harmonic content: Although the riff uses low Cs (the minor third) throughout, the tonality is deliberately ambiguous due to the use of the A5 chord with its omitted third.

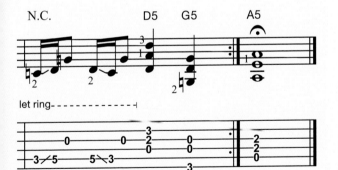

LICK NO. 1:

ROBIN TROWER-STYLE

Robin Trower was heavily influenced by Jimi Hendrix' overdriven sound and use of effects. This lick encapsulates Trower's wah-wah technique. Like Hendrix, Trower used the wah to create expressive vocal-like effects. The two basic wah-wah techniques are highlighted here: a slow sweep that adds vowel sounds to long notes; and a rocking motion (like tapping your foot to the beat) that adds a sweeping rhythmic effect.

Robin Trower at the UK's Reading Festival in the 1970s

RIFF REGISTER

Function: Multipurpose phrase that can be used either mid-solo or as a solo opening lick.

Technique: Sweeping and rhythmic wah-wah techniques that both begin with the pedal in the up position.

EDCAG position: Shape 1 tonic minor pentatonic.

Harmonic content: Typical minor pentatonic blues rock solo that's played in a power trio setting (i.e., without harmonic accompaniment).

WATCH OUT FOR

THE OPENING UNISON BENDS. PLAY THE HIGHER NOTE WITH YOUR FIRST FINGER, BENDING THE LOWER WITH YOUR FIRST AND SECOND FINGERS.

LICK NO. 2:
BILLY GIBBONS-STYLE

Billy Gibbons's minimalist approach to
solos is a big part of the ZZ Top sound.
Every note is carefully chosen and phrased.
This leaves plenty of room for expressive
techniques such as vibrato, hammer-ons/
pull-offs, and string bending. Gibbons's
playing always contains notes that hint at
the underlying chord sequence—a legacy
of years of live improvising with just bass
and drums for accompaniment.

Billy Gibbons on the TV
show *The Tube*, 1983

WATCH OUT FOR
OVERBENDING THE QUARTER-TONE BENDS.
THESE SHOULD BE SUBTLE AND UNDERSTATED.

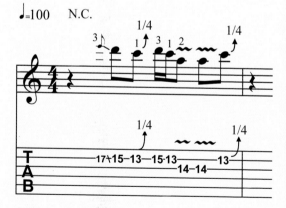

80

RIFF REGISTER

Function: Two-bar question-and-answer phrase that works well either as a fill between verses or a mid-solo lick.

Technique: Frequent use of quarter-tone bends and (controlled) vibrato that should be tastefully applied.

EDCAG position: Shape 4 tonic minor pentatonic concluding in shape 3 in the second bar.

Harmonic content: Minor pentatonic solo lick played over a minor pentatonic riff (in the studio) or against a bass and drums groove (live).

let ring - - -|

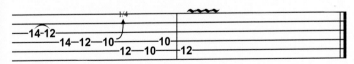

LICK NO. 3:

RORY GALLAGHER-STYLE

Rory Gallagher's tasteful and melodic soloing technique is one of the unsung highlights of 1970s rock music. He never overplayed in any of his solos, which are always melodic and full of feeling. This lick is a tribute to his total mastery of the instrument, and highlights his tasteful application of vibrato, precise bending technique, and rhythmic slurring.

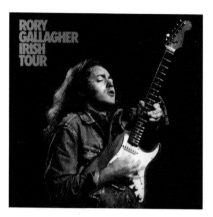

Album artwork for Rory Gallagher's *Irish Tour* (1974)

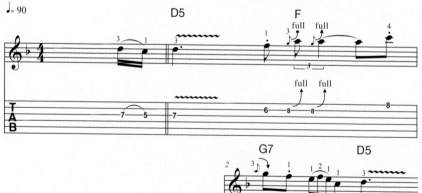

RIFF REGISTER

Function: Self-contained melodic statement that can be applied at any point in a solo.

Technique: Accurate tone bends are essential. Alternate sixteenth-note picking can be used throughout—it only needs to be applied to the last two notes in bar 2.

EDCAG position: Shape 4 tonic minor pentatonic with added major ninth (E) in the second bar.

Harmonic content: Minor pentatonic superimposed over tonic power chord, VI (F), and IV (G7). Notice how the relevant chord tones are applied to each chord using only the minor pentatonic.

WATCH OUT FOR

THE PRE-BEND AT THE START OF THE SECOND BAR. THE STRING MUST BE BENT UP A WHOLE STEP BEFORE IT'S PICKED AND RELEASED.

D5

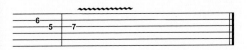

LICK NO. 4:
PAUL KOSSOFF-STYLE

Paul Kossoff's minimalist style and wide vibrato were legendary. Free's vocalist also played piano, which gave Kossoff more freedom when soloing. All the other guitarists in this section played in power trios, so when they took a solo there were no chords to accompany them. This affects note choices and changes the way you play—hence this Koss-style lick is the sparsest and most laid-back of the blues-rock licks featured here.

Paul Kossoff onstage with Free

WATCH OUT FOR
ALLOWING THE FRETTED THIRD STRING TO RING AGAINST THE OPEN STRING AT THE START OF THE SECOND BAR. THIS IS A CLASSIC KOSSOFF TRADEMARK.

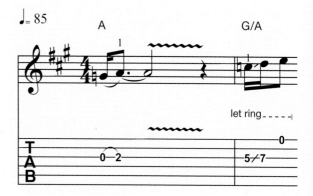

RIFF REGISTER

Function: Cool, understated two-bar phrase that is ideal as a solo opener.

Technique: Use a BB King style vibrato (but with the thumb on the neck) to add a gentle shimmering to the first note.

EDCAG position: Shape 5 minor pentatonic moving to shape 1 in the second bar.

Harmonic content: Tonic minor pentatonic phrase superimposed over a major chord sequence.

LICK NO. 1:
MAJOR CHORD VAMP

Eric Clapton's influence on rock guitar
style has been phenomenal. He was
the first player to push a Marshall amp
into overdrive, and was responsible for
elevating the status of the lead guitarist
within a band. This lick is typical of
Clapton's mid-1970s output as a solo
artist. It was during this period that he
recorded and performed with his famous
Fender Stratocaster, "Blackie."

Eric Clapton's hybrid
Stratocaster "Blackie"

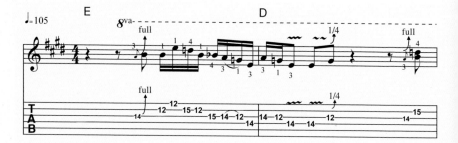

ERIC CLAPTON-STYLE LICKS

RIFF REGISTER

Function: Mid-solo lick or fill during instrumental section (i.e., between verses).

Technique: Tight, rhythmic lick that demands a confident alternate sixteenth-note picking technique.

EDCAG position: Shape 1 blues scale.

Harmonic content: Forces minor pentatonic/blues scale over a major vamp based on the chords I (E) and bVII (D).

WATCH OUT FOR

THE DOUBLE-STOP BEND LEADING INTO THE LAST BAR. USE THE FOURTH FINGER FOR THE HIGHER NOTE AND USE THREE FINGERS TO BEND THE LOWER.

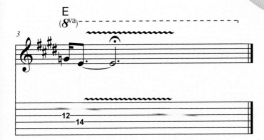

LICK NO. 2:
DOMINANT SEVENTH GROOVE

Eric Clapton formed Cream, the world's first supergroup, with Jack Bruce and Ginger Baker in 1966. Although the band was active for just two years, they changed the course of rock music forever. Clapton's blues pedigree shone through in all his work with Cream, the group that catapulted him to international superstar status. This Clapton-style lick is reminiscent of his fiery, yet perfectly phrased, soloing during this period.

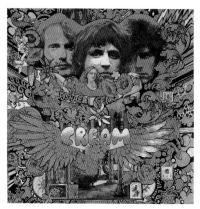

Album artwork for Cream's *Disraeli Gears* (1967)

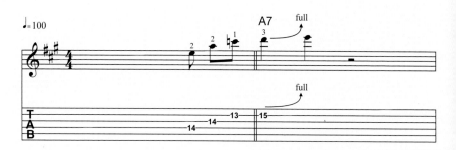

ERIC CLAPTON-STYLE LICKS

RIFF REGISTER

Function: Solo opening lick in classic blues-rock style.

Technique: The big two-step (major third) bend that opens this lick requires a confident string bending technique. Use three fingers to push the string up toward you.

EDCAG position: Shape 4 minor pentatonic opening phrase; moves down the neck to shape 1 in bar 2.

Harmonic content: Minor third is used to create a "blue note" over the tonic dominant seventh chord. The opening two-step bend briefly superimposes the thirteenth interval (F#) over the vamp.

WATCH OUT FOR

HITTING THE PITCH OF THAT BIG BEND AT THE START OF THE FIRST BAR. CHECK YOUR TARGET PITCH BY PLAYING THE F# ON THE NINETEENTH FRET BEFORE YOU BEND THE STRING.

A7

LICK NO. 3:
ROCK BALLAD-STYLE

Eric Clapton is no stranger to the ballad. Two of his hits, "Wonderful Tonight" and "Tears In Heaven," are still part of the rock repertoire. Ballads demand a melodic approach to soloing and many players write their ballad solos in advance rather than improvising. This lick is inspired by Clapton's work with Derek and the Dominoes in the early 1970s, an album that hinted at the direction his songwriting would take.

Clapton performing with
Derek And The Dominoes in
Connecticut, 1970

ERIC CLAPTON-STYLE LICKS

RIFF REGISTER

Function: Climactic two-bar phrase that concludes an eight-bar solo section (you can hear the second chorus beginning on the recording of this lick as the track fades).

Technique: Accurate, rhythmic sliding is required in the second bar to make this lick work.

EDCAG position: Shape 1 F# minor pentatonic. Sliding phrase descends then ascends through F# aeolian mode (natural minor) on first string.

Harmonic content: The tonic minor pentatonic and aeolian mode are used to create a melodic lick over an involved bIII, bII, bVI, and bVII sequence in F# minor.

WATCH OUT FOR

THE SLIDING PHRASE IN THE SECOND BAR. USE YOUR FIRST FINGER AS INDICATED, MAKING SURE YOU KEEP YOUR FINGER FIRMLY PRESSED DOWN AS YOU SLIDE.

LICK NO. 4:

MINIMALIST REGGAE-STYLE

Clapton's 1974 album *461 Ocean Boulevard*
was a radical move away from long guitar
solos. He had refocused his attention on
songwriting, and the album was a showcase
for his vocal talents. It included a cover of
Bob Marley's "I Shot The Sheriff," which
gave Clapton his first USA number 1 and
brought the previously unknown reggae
artist to the world. This lick is reminiscent
of Clapton's understated soloing technique
during this period.

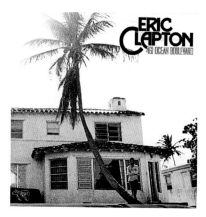

Album artwork for
461 Ocean Boulevard

WATCH OUT FOR

ALLOW THE OPENING NOTES ON THE
SECOND BEAT TO RING INTO EACH OTHER. USE
THREE FINGERS TO EXECUTE THE BEND.

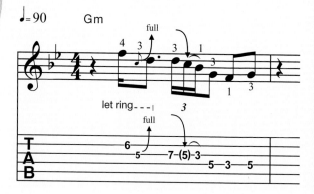

ERIC CLAPTON-STYLE LICKS

RIFF REGISTER

Function: Two-bar question-and-answer phrase that works as a solo lick or vocal chorus fill.

Technique: A good sense of time is required to be able to confidently avoid playing on the first beat of each bar.

EDCAG position: Shape 1 minor pentatonic lick.

Harmonic content: Minor seventh (F) is repeatedly used to create motion within the lick since it "pulls" back to the tonic (G).

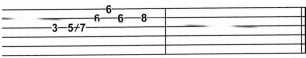

RIFF NO. 1:
DRIVING SIXTEENTH NOTES

Jimmy Page's playing was fiery and fast. The four guys of Zep had a magical chemistry which made the band much more than the sum of its parts. Page's continual searching for new ideas and sounds meant the band were never starved of inspired riffs. This simple riff contrasts two stabbed power chords with a complex sixteenth-note riff in the second bar—typical of Page's work on the band's first album.

Jimmy Page in Australia, 1967, playing guitar with a violin bow

RIFF REGISTER

Function: Main riff that leaves space for virtuoso drum fills when used as an intro section.

Technique: Strict alternate sixteenth-note picking is required in the second bar.

EDCAG position: Shape 4 A5 chord followed by shape 1 G major pentatonic riff.

Harmonic content: I (A) to bVII (G) chord sequence with the second chord implied only by the notes of the riff.

WATCH OUT FOR

THE SLIGHTLY TRICKY PICKING AND FINGERING IN THE SECOND BAR. ALWAYS START SLOWLY!

RIFF NO. 2:

THE "DEAR PRUDENCE" SEQUENCE

Just about everybody in the 1960s had
a tune based on the Beatles song "Dear
Prudence"—essentially a repeated arpeggio
played against a descending bass line.
This example is a typical Page-style
interpretation of the "Dear Prudence"
sequence. In true Zeppelin style, a
distorted electric guitar replaces the gently
picked acoustic of the original.

Copenhagen, 1968: the
first performance by the
Led Zeppelin line-up

WATCH OUT FOR

FRETTING THE CHORD NOTES CLEANLY
WITHOUT INADVERTENTLY DAMPING
ADJACENT STRINGS.

RIFF REGISTER

Function: Hypnotic two-bar riff that functions well as a main riff or interlude section.

Technique: Precise fretting-hand technique is required to allow all the chord notes to ring clearly.

EDCAG position: Shape 4 tonic major chord-based riff.

Harmonic content: Although this riff is written in the major key, the major third of the B chord is never stated. This intentionally creates harmonic ambiguity.

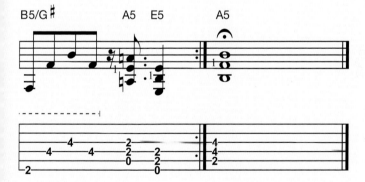

B5/G♯   A5   E5   A5

RIFF NO. 3:
ELECTRIC 12-STRING

Jimmy Page used any guitar he could lay his hands on during Zeppelin's recording career. Famed for playing his double-necked Gibson 6/12 string live, he also played electric 12-string in the studio. Listen carefully and you'll notice it's everywhere on Zeppelin recordings—think of the Byrds-like sound of "Thank You," the double-tracked riff of "Livin' Lovin' Maid," or the early Who vibe on "The Song Remains the Same."

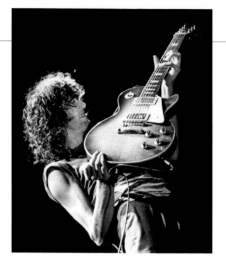

Jimmy Page onstage in Rotterdam, The Netherlands, 1980

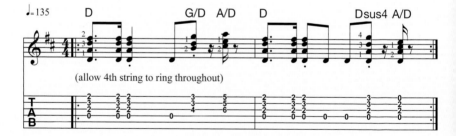

(allow 4th string to ring throughout)

RIFF REGISTER

Function: Syncopated, driving riff that functions as an instrumental interlude or solo accompaniment.

Technique: If you're playing this on a 12-string (it still sounds cool on a regular 6-string), a nimble fretting-hand technique is required.

EDCAG position: Shape 2 open position tonic major chord moving plus shape 1 triads (G and A).

Harmonic content: The continually ringing open D-string is a pedal bass note, which is also sounded against chords IV (G) and V (A) in addition to the tonic.

WATCH OUT FOR

ALLOWING THE OPEN FOURTH STRING TO RING CLEARLY THROUGHOUT. BE CAREFUL NOT TO DAMP IT WHEN CHANGING CHORDS.

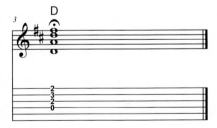

RIFF NO. 4:
LESS IS MORE

In his Led Zeppelin days, Jimmy Page was the master of the riff. He produced barnstorming power riffs from little more than a few pentatonic notes. The iconic riff in "Whole Lotta Love" has just four. "The Immigrant Song" or "The Wanton Song" have only two—the root and octave. This riff, in the style of Page's mid-Zep period, weighs in at four notes, with a couple of dominant seventh chords thrown in.

The American single cover for "Whole Lotta Love" (1969)

RIFF REGISTER

Function: Two-bar riff used as the main groove in a heavy rock song.

Technique: Alternate sixteenth-note picking should be used throughout (on the chords too).

EDCAG position: Shape 1 minor pentatonic.

Harmonic content: Ambiguous riff that vaguely outlines a tonic dominant seventh chord. The rising chords pull back to a "home" tonic dominant seventh that is never actually played.

WATCH OUT FOR

KEEPING ALL THE NOTES SHORT AND PERCUSSIVE. FRETTED NOTES ARE EASY TO DAMP BY SIMPLY RELEASING THE PRESSURE OF YOUR FINGER.

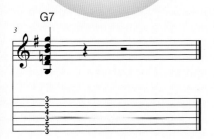

G7

LICK NO. 1:
SLICK PULL-OFF-STYLE

Page's lead work is sometimes dismissed as sloppy. Certainly, it deteriorated during his Led Zeppelin years, as the band's hedonistic lifestyle took its toll. But his early playing was precise, fiery, and intense—all qualities that the legions of one-dimensional shred players just don't have. This lick is typical of his work on Zeppelin's first album, released in 1969—regarded by many as the most important rock album ever made.

Cover art for Led Zeppelin's self-titled debut album

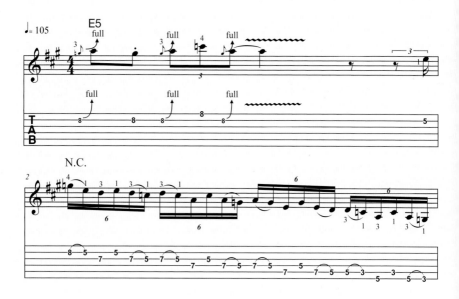

RIFF REGISTER

Function: Mid-solo, question-and-answer phrase lick.

Technique: Quick and accurate bends are contrasted with a fast pull-off-based lick.

EDCAG position: Shape 1 tonic minor pentatonic.

Harmonic content: Tonic minor pentatonic forced over a major key riff.

WATCH OUT FOR

KEEPING YOUR FIRST FINGER ON THE FRETBOARD IN THE SECOND BAR. DON'T MOVE YOUR FINGER UNTIL YOU PLAY THE LAST NOTE OF EACH SEXTUPLET.

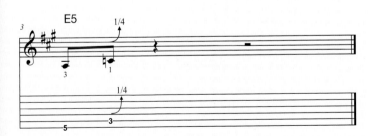

LICK NO. 2:
USING SIXTH INTERVALS

Page's influences included blues, rock & roll, and country players. This broad range of influences allowed him to cherry-pick the best bits of each genre. This lick opens with a classic sixths phrase; you will hear a similar use of them in the work of many players, from Chuck Berry to Steve Cropper. Page was never afraid to incorporate tried-and-true ideas in his solos.

Jimmy Page performing in Oakland, California, 1977, playing a Gibson Les Paul

RIFF REGISTER

Function: Major sixths are used to superimpose major tonality on a harmonically androgynous power chord riff.

Technique: Alternate sixteenth-note picking should be used throughout.

EDCAG position: Opens with major sixth from the shape 2 major pentatonic, moving to shape 3 by the end of the first bar.

Harmonic content: Simple power chord riff has its major tonality confirmed by a major pentatonic-based solo.

WATCH OUT FOR

ALLOWING THE OPENING NOTES TO SUSTAIN INTO EACH OTHER—JUST LIKE PICKING THE NOTES OUT OF AN OPEN CHORD.

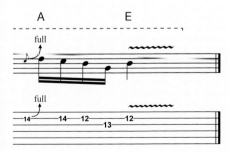

LICK NO. 3:
MOTIF-BASED PHRASE

Motifs are short melodic fragments. By restating a motif
with variation (either by starting on a different step
of the scale or changing the rhythm slightly), fluent
improvisers add phrasing and continuity to their solos.
Without motifs, a solo is merely a meaningless collection
of scale notes. Jimmy Page is a very melodic player and
frequently creates his solos from short motifs, particularly
when starting a solo. This lick repeats the idea contained
in the first bar but starts it on the fifth of the scale in the
second bar to create a melodic solo opener.

Press ad for Zeppelin's
Houses of the Holy
album (1973)

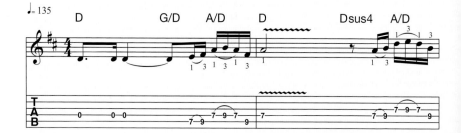

RIFF REGISTER

Function: Two-bar question-and-answer opening phrase, based on a repeated motif.

Technique: Strong hammer-on/pull-off technique required for the slurred notes at the end of each bar.

EDCAG position: Shape 5 tonic major pentatonic scale.

Harmonic content: A straightforward major key chord vamp with solo derived from the corresponding major pentatonic.

WATCH OUT FOR

LETTING THE FIRST NOTE OF EACH BAR RING. THIS CREATES CONTRAST WITH THE SIXTEENTH-NOTE PHRASE AT THE END OF EACH BAR.

LICK NO. 4:
COUNTRY-STYLE-BENDS

Page often played country-style licks in his Zeppelin solos, especially in the latter part of the band's career when he started using a Fender Telecaster with a "B bender." The double-stop bend is a mainstay of country music vocabulary because it mimics the sound of a pedal steel guitar. The double stop bend should be infused with a healthy dose of distortion to recreate Page's trademark sound.

Jimmy Page performing in Oakland, California, 1977, playing a twin-necked Gibson EDS-1275

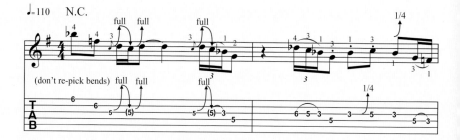

RIFF REGISTER

Function: Country-flavored solo opening lick.

Technique: Good finger independence, particularly in the fourth finger to allow the upper note to remain constant while the lower is bent up a tone.

EDCAG position: Shape 1 minor pentatonic.

Harmonic content: Double-stop bend creates the upper minor third of a close position dominant seventh chord.

WATCH OUT FOR

ACCURATE BENDING WITH THE THIRD FINGER. USE YOUR FIRST AND SECOND FINGERS BEHIND THE THIRD TO INCREASE STRENGTH.

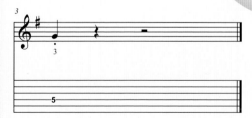

RIFF NO. 1:
THE HENDRIX CHORD

Although Hendrix didn't actually invent the 7#9 chord (jazz musicians had been using it for decades), he did popularize its use in rock music. By adding a sharpened (augmented) ninth to a dominant seventh, a harmonically ambiguous chord is produced. Because the raised ninth is the enharmonic equivalent of a minor third, you could say it's a dominant chord with both major and minor thirds.

Cover art of the Jimi Hendrix Experience's 1968 compilation album, *Smash Hits*

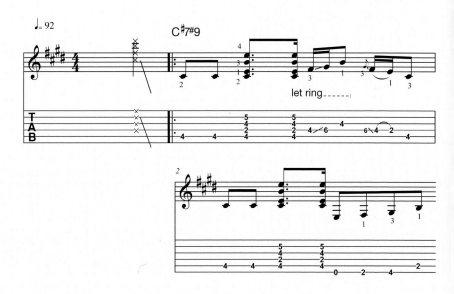

RIFF REGISTER

Function: Main riff used as an instrumental intro/interlude. Riffs such as these would often be simplified when used as a vocal or solo accompaniment.

Technique: Alternate sixteenth-note picking and accurate, rhythmic sliding.

EDCAG position: Shape 4 chord with shape 3 and 4 minor pentatonic scale for the riff.

Harmonic content: Augmented ninth blurs major tonality of dominant seventh sound by adding what is effectively the minor third to the chord.

WATCH OUT FOR

STARTING THE SLIDE IN THE FIRST BAR WITH YOUR THIRD FINGER. ALTHOUGH IT'S TEMPTING TO USE YOUR SECOND, THIS WILL PUT YOUR HAND IN THE WRONG POSITION FOR THE REMAINING NOTES.

RIFF NO. 2:

REVERSE II–V SEQUENCE

The 1960s was a time of musical experimentation. In the first half of the decade people like The Beach Boys and the Motown songwriters were pushing the boundaries of pop harmony. By the end of the decade, nobody could match Hendrix' maverick approach. This Hendrix-style riff is based on a reversal of the II–V chord progression beloved by jazz musicians.

Hendrix live onstage in Paris, 1967, playing a white Fender Stratocaster

WATCH OUT FOR

MAINTAINING A PENDULUM-LIKE, EIGHTH NOTE, RIGHT-HAND MOVEMENT THROUGHOUT. THIS HELPS TO ACHIEVE A SOLID GROOVE WHEN MIXING CHORDS AND SINGLE NOTES.

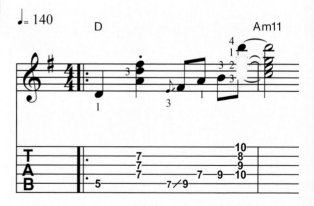

RIFF REGISTER

Function: Two-bar riff that outlines the underlying harmonic sequence with a mixture of chords and notes.

Technique: Alternate eighth-note picking should be used throughout.

EDCAG position: Shape 4 major chord (V) shape followed by shape 2 minor chord (II).

Harmonic content: Based on a II–V sequence in the key of G major. By reversing the progression a suspended (9sus4) dominant (V) sound is implied in the second bar.

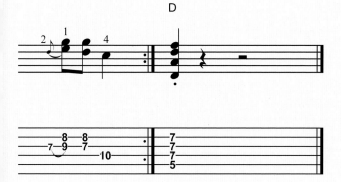

RIFF NO. 3:
USING CHORD EMBELLISHMENT

Jimi Hendrix cut his teeth on the USA's chitlin' circuit as a rhythm guitarist for various R&B acts. During this time he developed his formidable rhythm guitar style. The sophisticated techniques used in R&B became the mainstay of Hendrix' rock rhythm technique. This example illustrates how a simple chord progression can be transformed into an unmistakably Hendrix-style riff with nothing more than a little embellishment.

Curtis Knight and The Squires (Jimi Hendrix second from left), 1966

J I M I   H E N D R I X - S T Y L E   R I F F S

RIFF REGISTER

Function: Two-bar chord sequence harmonized with embellished chords and a double-stop riff.

Technique: Independent (from the other fingers) and agile use of the fretting hand's fourth finger.

EDCAG position: Shape 4 open chord (Am) followed by shape 1

semi-barre chord (G) and a shape 3 double-stop riff.

Harmonic content: Basic chord shapes are enhanced by trilling a diatonic note above a chord note while holding down the full chord. The fourth (D) is briefly sounded against Am and the ninth (A) against G.

WATCH OUT FOR

GETTING YOUR FOURTH FINGER TO WORK INDEPENDENTLY OF YOUR OTHER THREE FINGERS. PRACTISE EACH CHORD IDEA SEPARATELY AND SLOWLY.

Am

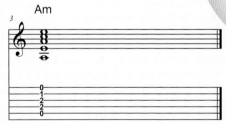

RIFF NO. 4:
SIMPLE PENTATONIC RIFF

Although Hendrix was not afraid to use dense harmonic textures and intricate chordal embellishments, he never shunned the simple or obvious. Some of his most memorable riffs consisted of nothing more than a few minor pentatonic notes. Notice how the phrase in the second bar is rhythmically identical to the first, and how the notes form an ascending and descending wave pattern on the stave.

Cover art for Hendrix'
Are You Experienced
album (1967)

JIMI HENDRIX-STYLE RIFFS

RIFF REGISTER

Function: Simple two-bar riff that works well as an intro or instrumental interlude.

Technique: Alternate eighth-note picking and a controlled bending technique.

EDCAG position: Shape 3 minor pentatonic.

Harmonic content: Although this is a simple pentatonic riff without any harmonic accompaniment, each phrase ends on the root note—leaving the listener in no doubt of the basic tonality.

WATCH OUT FOR

ALLOWING THE SECOND AND THIRD NOTES (ON THE SAME FRET) TO RING INTO EACH OTHER. ROLL YOUR FIRST FINGER ACROSS THE STRINGS AS YOU PLAY THE NOTES.

E7#9

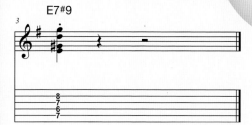

LICK NO. 1:
PRE-BENDING TECHNIQUE

Jimi Hendrix took the guitar's expressive
potential to its limit. Disparate effects had
been trialed since the 1940s; but only Hendrix
combined the heady mix of string bending,
whammy bar, distortion, and effects to achieve
new levels of expression on the instrument. It's
difficult to appreciate today just how Hendrix
blew everyone away when he burst onto an
unsuspecting London music scene in 1966.

Hendrix playing guitar
with his teeth in Fillmore
East, New York, 1968

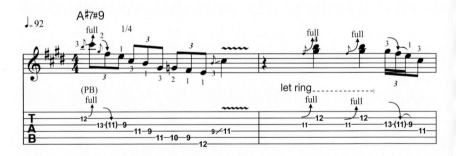

JIMI HENDRIX - STYLE LICKS

RIFF REGISTER

Function: Opening lick for solo based on a "Hendrix chord" vamp.

Technique: Accurate bending technique involving pre-bends and double-stop bends.

EDCAG position: Shape 1 minor pentatonic/blues scale.

Harmonic content: Pre-bends highlight the root (C#) and fifth (G#) of the tonic dominant seventh. Blues scale perfectly outlines the tense-sounding dominant 7#9 chord.

WATCH OUT FOR

ACCURATE PITCHING OF THE PRE-BENDS. USING THE FINGERS INDICATED, YOU SHOULD BE ABLE TO PRE-BEND BOTH NOTES SIMULTANEOUSLY.

LICK NO. 2:
SUCCESSIVE REPEATED BENDS

In Hendrix' hands the guitar screamed, shouted, and cried. He used every expressive technique he could, quite literally, get his hands on. His string-bending skill helped him to create emotional, vocal-like sounds. This lick illustrates a simple but effective technique: the repeated string bend. Repeating the same bend several times emulates the most emotional of all sounds—a human cry.

The guitar which Hendrix famously set aflame at the London Astoria in 1967

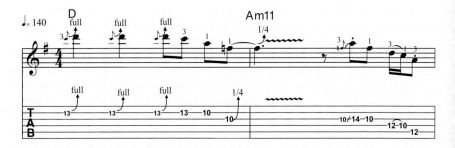

RIFF REGISTER

Function: Simple but powerful solo opening lick based on a repeated string bend.

Technique: Accurate whole-step bending technique is needed to ensure repeated bends are in tune.

EDCAG position: Shape 1 minor pentatonic.

Harmonic content: Minor pentatonic lick that "ignores" the second chord (Am11) and forces D minor pentatonic over both chords. This technique works because the phrase is strong and focuses the listener's ear on the tonic (D) chord tonality.

WATCH OUT FOR

HITTING REPEATED BENDS PITCH-PERFECT. USE YOUR FIRST AND SECOND FINGERS BEHIND THE THIRD TO INCREASE BENDING POWER.

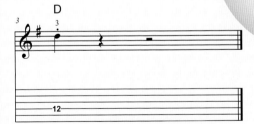

LICK NO. 3:
MINOR THIRD BENDS

One of the reasons Hendrix drop-tuned his guitar a half-step (low to high: Eb–Ab–Db–Gb–Bb–Eb) was to enable him to bend the strings more easily. Drop-tuning the guitar was nothing new, and neither were large interval bends, but Hendrix somehow made everything he did sound completely his own. This lick opens with a repeated minor third (one and a half step) bend, a sound that can be heard in many of Hendrix' solos.

Cover of the 1968
Hendrix album
Electric Ladyland

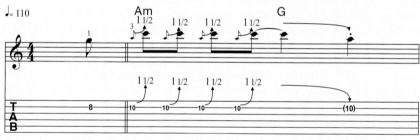

J I M I H E N D R I X - S T Y L E L I C K S

RIFF REGISTER

Function: Fiery, intense, two-bar lick; works best as a solo opener.

Technique: Strong left-hand technique is required to achieve accurate bends.

EDCAG position: Shape 2 minor pentatonic moving to shape 1 blues scale.

Harmonic content: One and a half step bend raises tonic pitch to the minor third (second step of the minor pentatonic). Because this chord progression is diatonic, the tonic minor pentatonic/blues scale can be applied to all the chords.

WATCH OUT FOR

BUILDING STRENGTH GRADUALLY. PRACTICE BENDING MINOR THIRDS FREQUENTLY FOR SHORT PERIODS TO BUILD FINGER MUSCLES AND AVOID STRAINING YOUR FINGERS.

Am

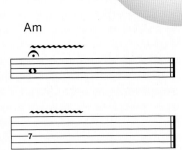

LICK NO. 4:
USING COLOR TONES

Color tones are the notes of the scale that aren't present in the chord. There are only three color tones in any seven-note scale or mode: the second (ninth), sixth (thirteenth), and fourth (eleventh). These notes will have most impact when played against a chord. The unusual effect on the CD is a Roger Mayer Octavia pedal—an effect developed specifically for Hendrix in 1967.

Hendrix' Marshall amp
and Univibe guitar
effects pedal

RIFF REGISTER

Function: Two-bar, mid-solo lick; also works well between verses.

Technique: Accurate hammer-ons/ pull-offs to generate the upper notes of the trills. Quick and precise one-string slides (harder than it sounds!).

EDCAG position: Shape 1 dorian mode moving to shape 4 in bar 2.

Harmonic content: Superimposes the major sixth and major ninth over a static dominant vamp. Although these intervals don't really work against the chord, since they're briefly oscillated with a chord tone, they are an effective use of color tones.

WATCH OUT FOR

SLIDING DOWN THE SECOND STRING QUICKLY AND ACCURATELY. USE YOUR FIRST FINGER FOR ALL THE SLIDES AS INDICATED.

RIFF NO. 1:

STEVE HOWE-STYLE

Steve Howe joined Yes in 1970 just
before the release of the acclaimed *The
Yes Album.* Howe was equally adept at
finger-style acoustic work and playing
long, jazz-inspired solos. Many regard Yes
as the pioneers of prog rock. Their work
remains an inspiration for bands such as
Dream Theater and Spock's Beard. The
swirling effect on the accompanying CD is
a phaser—an early modulation effect pedal.

Steve Howe onstage at London's
Wembley Arena, 1978

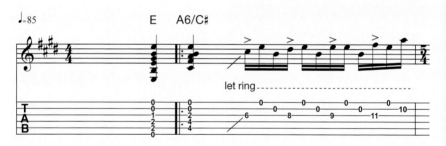

PROG ROCK-STYLE RIFFS

RIFF REGISTER

Function: Opening instrumental section that states the main motif of the song.

Technique: Can be played finger-style (using p m i), pick-style (with alternate picking), or with hybrid picking (playing the third string with the pick and using a and m for the higher notes).

EDCAG position: Rhythmic pattern that ascends from E major shape 3 to shape 5 using open strings.

Harmonic content: Picking pattern superimposes tensions both rhythmically and harmonically against a static IV (A) chord. The major 6, 7, and 9, plus the augmented 11, are all incorporated.

WATCH OUT FOR

THE RHYTHMIC COMPLEXITY OF THIS RIFF. NOT ONLY DOES IT ALTERNATE BETWEEN 4/4 AND 5/4, THE SIXTEENTH-NOTE PICKING PATTERN IS PLAYED IN ACCENTED GROUPS OF THREE AGAINST THE BEAT.

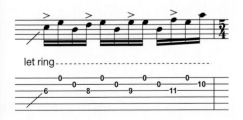

RIFF NO. 2:

TREVOR RABIN-STYLE

In 1981 Yes disbanded, but they reformed
two years later with Trevor Rabin on
guitar. Their first single, "Owner Of A
Lonely Heart," taken from the album
90125, won the band many new, younger
fans, thanks to its mix of contemporary
production, in-your-face rock guitar
sound, and vocal harmonies. The effect
you can hear on the CD is a flanger—a
popular effect with rock guitarists during
the 1980s.

Trevor Rabin onstage in
New York, 1987

WATCH OUT FOR

HOLDING DOWN CHORD SHAPES
THROUGHOUT—DON'T MAKE THE
MISTAKE OF PLAYING SINGLE-NOTE
ARPEGGIO PATTERNS.

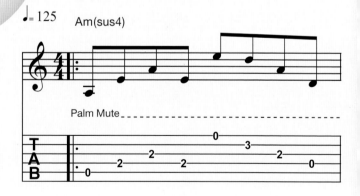

RIFF REGISTER

Function: Percussive arpeggio-based riff ideal for accompaniment in verse sections.

Technique: An accurate alternate eighth-note picking is required for the tricky string jumps.

EDCAG position: Based on shape 4 A minor chord. Moves to a shape 3 major arpeggio shape in bar 2.

Harmonic content: The added D note in the first bar replaces the minor third of the chord and creates that all-important harmonic ambiguity. It's this quality that gives the riff its edgy sound.

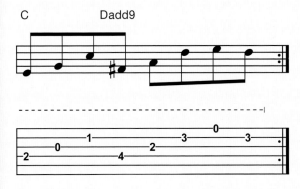

RIFF NO. 3:
STEVE HACKETT-STYLE

The original Genesis line-up of the early 1970s featured the talents of vocalist Peter Gabriel and guitarist Steve Hackett. Hackett's work was subtle, melodic, and influenced by classical music. Hackett was expert at creating subtle textures with both acoustic and electric guitars. He often used a 12-string electric, a distinctive habit that remained part of the Genesis sound long after his departure from the group in 1977.

Genesis performing in Cleveland, Ohio, 1973

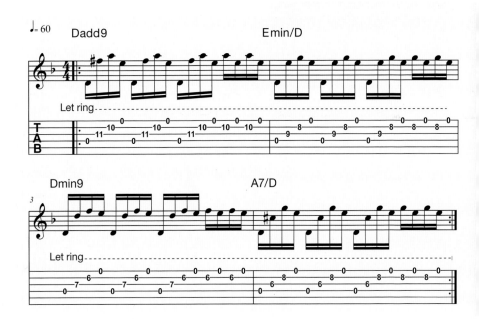

RIFF REGISTER

Function: Opening motif and ideal vocal accompaniment for verse sections.

Technique: Can be played pick-style (using alternate sixteenth-note picking), or finger-style (using a p i p m picking pattern).

EDCAG position: Shape 1 major chord fragment that descends to shape 4 minor.

Harmonic content: Uses major and minor tonality to create a pseudo-classical texture. The dominant seventh chord (A7) sounded against the tonic pedal is a common feature of classical guitar repertoire.

WATCH OUT FOR

MAINTAINING A CONSISTENT AND ACCURATE PICKING PATTERN THROUGHOUT. CRESCENDO AND DIMINUENDO TECHNIQUES SHOULD BE APPLIED ONCE YOU'RE CONFIDENT WITH THE PICKING.

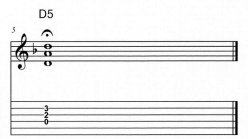

D5

RIFF NO. 4:
DAVE GILMOUR-STYLE

This Pink Floyd style riff is typical of the band's work during the early 1970s—a period many regard as the band's best. Gilmour was head and shoulders above his peers when it came to creating melodic, soaring lead lines. The pulsating effect you can hear on the CD was created with a tremolo pedal. This effect, originally a feature of Fender amplifiers, is created with amplitude modulation (a repeated increase and decrease in volume).

Dave Gilmour playing a Fender Telecaster Custom in New York's Nassau Coliseum, 1975

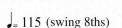

RIFF REGISTER

Function: Two-bar riff that adds a twist to the classic pentatonic sound by using an odd time signature.

Technique: Use down-picks throughout except for the third note; since this is an off-beat eighth note, it should be picked upward.

EDCAG position: Shape 4 A minor pentatonic.

Harmonic content: Apart from the use of the quarter-tone bend that pulls the riff back to the start, the riff uses only notes from the A minor pentatonic against an A minor 7 chord. It's the unusual meter that makes the riff sound special.

WATCH OUT FOR

GETTING THE 7/4 GROOVE! TRY COUNTING THIS AS IF IT WERE A BAR OF 4/4 FOLLOWED BY A BAR OF 3/4—YOU WILL FIND THIS FEELS MORE NATURAL AND YOU WILL SOON BE ABLE TO PLAY WITHOUT COUNTING AT ALL.

Amin

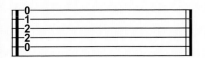

LICK NO. 1:
DOUBLE TRACKED LICK

Dave Gilmour's guitar-playing is always tasteful; he uses effects musically, not for their own sake. He experimented with a studio effect called ADT (automatic double tracking). This effect was developed at Abbey Road Studios, where Floyd recorded their famous *Dark Side of the Moon* album. It sounds like two guitars playing the same notes simultaneously, and produces a huge soundscape—perfectly suited to Gilmour's long sustained notes and minimalist style.

Abbey Road Studios, London

DAVE GILMOUR-STYLE LICKS

RIFF REGISTER

Function: Opening solo lick over tonic minor vamp.

Technique: Accurate bending is required, particularly for the long sustained opening note.

EDCAG position: Shape 1 B minor pentatonic with the descending

phrase in the penultimate bar moving to shape five.

Harmonic content: Long notes focus on chord tones (i.e., the root and minor third). The closing line introduces chromaticism between the minor third and root note.

WATCH OUT FOR
ACCURATE BENDING! THERE'S NOTHING WORSE THAN HITTING A BIG BEND FLAT OR SHARP, ESPECIALLY WHEN IT'S THE FIRST NOTE OF YOUR SOLO.

Bmin7

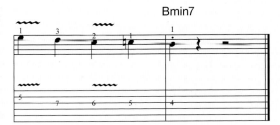

LICK NO. 2:
BLUESY PHRASING

There's no denying the heavy blues influence in Dave Gilmour's technique. His mastery of the blues vocabulary is never used in predictable settings. Often his bluesiest work with Floyd served as the perfect foil to what could otherwise have become an overindulgent prog rock synth-fest! His bending technique is clean and precise and always pitch-perfect, as this Gilmour style lick illustrates.

Album cover for Pink Floyd's *Wish You Were Here* (1975)

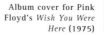

RIFF REGISTER

Function: Ideal prog rock intro.

Technique: Strong and accurate bending required, particularly in bar 2 where the note is bent up a tone, released and re-bent up two tones.

EDCAG position: G minor pentatonic shape 1 (first at the fifteenth fret and concluding an octave lower) with bar 2 dipping briefly into shape 5.

Harmonic content: G minor pentatonic scale notes super-imposed over Ebmaj7 and D7. Although this shouldn't work over the dominant chord, the cadential quality of the final lick emphasizes the V–I progression perfectly.

WATCH OUT FOR

HOLDING DOWN CHORD SHAPES THROUGH-OUT—DON'T MAKE THE MISTAKE OF PLAYING SINGLE-NOTE ARPEGGIO PATTERNS.

Gmin

LICK NO. 3:
INCORPORATING DOUBLE STOPS

Like many players, Dave Gilmour frequently uses bluesy double-stop licks. Double stops are simply two notes played simultaneously, so they are perfect for reinforcing the harmony of a solo. In this example they are used to separate two sixteenth-note licks, and contrast the more intricate phrases with an instantly recognizable slice of raw blues grunt. It's this ability to mix common vocabulary with original ideas that sets the truly great players apart.

Poster for the Pink Floyd film *The Wall*

DAVE GILMOUR-STYLE LICKS

RIFF REGISTER

Function: Opening solo lick in a question-and-answer form that's punctuated by the double-stop phrase.

Technique: Playing major third (as in this example) double stops is easy on the second and third strings—you simply barre across the strings with one finger as indicated.

EDCAG position: Primarily shape 1 minor pentatonic with notes added above and below from shapes 2 and 5.

Harmonic content: The double stop on the twelfth fret lingers on the perfect fourth and major sixth to create tension before resolving back to the minor third and perfect fourth.

WATCH OUT FOR

THAT BIG MAJOR THIRD (TWO WHOLE TONES) BEND IN BAR 4. ALL THE NOTES ARE GENERATED BY BENDING THE STRING ONLY— DON'T RE-PICK THE STRING AFTER PLAYING THE FIRST NOTE.

LICK NO. 4:

USING ORNAMENTATION

In this example a mordent is used at the start of bar 1 to highlight the sound of the major ninth. A mordent is a short trill that quickly alternates a note with one directly above or below it. Both chromatic (half-step) and diatonic (using only notes from the scale) mordents are used. In guitar music, the notes are usually written in the stave (especially when using TAB with conventional notation).

Cover art for Pink Floyd's *The Dark Side of the Moon* (1973)

RIFF REGISTER

Function: Two-bar lick that provides a solo ending since it descends cadential-style to the root note (D).

Technique: Quick, precise hammer-on/pull-off technique is required to play mordents and trills effectively.

EDCAG position: Shape 1 D minor pentatonic.

Harmonic content: Because the major ninth (E) is present in the C/D chord, the ninth fits perfectly over this chord when it is emphasized by the mordent in bar 1. Although this chord symbol implies a D11 chord, this would function as the second chord in a D minor vamp, so the harmony is firmly rooted in D minor.

WATCH OUT FOR

BEING PULLED OUT OF POSITION BY YOUR FIRST FINGER ON THE NINTH FRET. NOTICE THAT THE FOLLOWING NOTE (D) ON THE FOURTH STRING IS PLAYED WITH YOUR THIRD FINGER TO RETURN YOUR HAND TO TENTH POSITION.

Dm

RIFF NO. 1:
DEEP PURPLE-STYLE

Deep Purple guitarist Ritchie Blackmore
penned what is possibly the most copied
riff of all time: "Smoke On The Water." It's
impossible to get anywhere close to that
iconic riff without sounding like a poor
imitation. So this riff is based on Blackmore's
bluesy, single-note style riffs, which were the
basis for many other classic Purple tracks.
Notice that the organ and the bass also double
up the riff—an important element of the
Purple sound.

Ritchie Blackmore swinging a
smashed guitar; on tour in the USA,
1974

RIFF REGISTER

Function: Main riff in a classic rock-style tune. Usually featured as an intro and may also be used as the basis of the song's chorus.

Technique: Finger rolling is required to play notes quickly and accurately when they fall on the same fret (i.e., the last two notes in the first bar).

EDCAG position: Shape 3 E minor pentatonic.

Harmonic content: Although written in the key of E minor, the tonic minor chord is never actually played to preserve the sense of harmonic ambiguity.

WATCH OUT FOR

THE QUICK SHIFT FROM THE LOW B AT THE END OF THE THIRD BAR TO THE D5 IN THE FOLLOWING BAR. PLAY BOTH THE B AND THE LOWEST NOTE OF THE CHORD WITH YOUR FIRST FINGER.

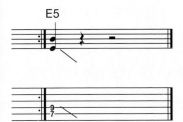

E5

RIFF NO. 2:
URIAH HEEP-STYLE

Formed in 1969, Uriah Heep were pioneers of the British heavy rock movement. Like Deep Purple, their sound was based on a blend of overdriven organ and distorted guitar. Their riff-based tunes were interlaced with dense vocal harmonies, earning them the nickname "The Beach Boys of heavy metal." Guitarist Mick Box is the only original member still in the band's' current line-up. They are still touring and recording after more than 40 years in the business.

Mick Box performing
live onstage, 1995

RIFF REGISTER

Function: Two-bar intro riff punctuated with stops to create a sense of anticipation before the song begins.

Technique: Alternate sixteenth-note picking is required throughout.

EDCAG position: Shape 3 (open position) C minor pentatonic.

Harmonic content: Minor seventh, minor third, and perfect fourth are each stated, followed by three tonic notes. Although the perfect fourth is not a chord tone, it can always be safely added to the minor chord.

WATCH OUT FOR

PLAYING THE REPEATED SIXTEENTH NOTES EVENLY AND CONSISTENTLY WITH ALTERNATE PICKING TO CREATE A DRIVING GROOVE.

C5

RIFF NO. 3:
QUEEN-STYLE

It's easy to forget just how hard Queen could rock when they wanted to. Queen's early work, and in particular their third album, *Sheer Heart Attack* (1974) is hard rock at its hardest. The band became famous for their multi-tracked vocals and guitar parts, but check out this album if you've never heard guitarist Brian May rocking out. As testament to this, both Def Leppard and Metallica have recorded covers of Queen's early material.

Queen in Copenhagen, 1974

H E A V Y R O C K - S T Y L E R I F F S

RIFF REGISTER

Function: Big-sounding, open E riff used as an instrumental break after chorus sections.

Technique: Some deft fingerwork and string jumping required to make this riff sound relaxed at 132 bpm.

EDCAG position: Based on lower notes of E mixolydian mode, shape 2.

Harmonic content: Chromatic approach note (G) played before the major third (G#) heightens the major quality. This is contrasted in the second bar by the low, non-diatonic G5 power chord. Like many cool bluesy riffs, this one weaves in and out of major and minor tonality.

WATCH OUT FOR

THE JUMP FROM THE LOW G# TO THE D5 AT THE END OF THE FIRST BAR. USE YOUR FIRST AND FOURTH FINGERS TO FRET THE D5 AS INDICATED.

E5

RIFF NO. 4:
MOUNTAIN-STYLE

Mountain were a hugely influential American heavy rock band. They achieved success in a scene dominated by British groups in the late 1960s and early 1970s. Mountain's guitarist and vocalist, Leslie West, has continued to front various incarnations of the band, who are still performing and recording. West was famous for his thick, overdriven sound and his frequent use of power chord-based riffs.

Mountain in 1971

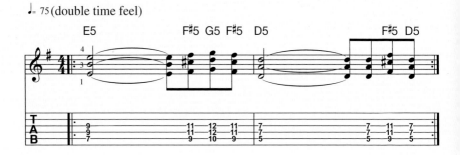

H E A V Y R O C K - S T Y L E R I F F S

RIFF REGISTER

Function: Mid-song riff that pushes a rock ballad into hard rock territory with a double-time riff.

Technique: Accurate fretting of these swift-moving, three-note power chord shapes is essential for creating a big sound.

EDCAG position: Shape 4 power chord moved up and down the fifth string.

Harmonic content: Parallel motion (i.e., each note moves the same distance) of these power chords creates the non-diatonic F#5 chord—adding tension which is relieved by sustained E5 and D5 chords.

WATCH OUT FOR

KEEPING YOUR THIRD FINGER CLOSE TO THE FRET AT ALL TIMES. IF THIS FINGER IS FRETTED LAZILY, THERE'S A DANGER THAT THE DIMINISHED FIFTH INTERVAL COULD BE GENERATED, WHICH WON'T SOUND GOOD.

RIFF NO. 1:
USING TWO-NOTE POWER CHORDS

Black Sabbath's guitarist Tony Iommi pioneered the heavy, drop-tuned style used by today's modern metal bands. As a teenager, Iommi lost the tips of two of his right-hand fingers (he's left-handed) in an accident at the factory where he worked. By wearing thimbles fashioned out of detergent bottles, he was able to play again. Lowered tunings also helped him to play more easily since the tension of the strings was greatly reduced.

Tony Iommi at London's
Alexandra Palace Festival, 1973

TONY IOMMI-STYLE RIFFS

RIFF REGISTER

Function: Main riff in a heavy rock-style tune. Frequently Sabbath tunes used riffs such as this for both the intro and verse.

Technique: Two-note power chords are used, since they are more "mobile" than the three-note variety.

EDCAG position: Shape 4 power chord (with root on the fifth string).

Harmonic content: Although this chord sequence is based on the key of C# minor, the percussive chord on the second beat is played by barring across the ninth fret and states the major third of the chord.

WATCH OUT FOR

KEEPING THE CHORD SHAPE INTACT
AS YOU SLIDE DOWN TO A5 ON THE
SECOND FRET.

C#5

RIFF NO. 2:
USING DROP-TUNED OPEN CHORDS

All the examples in this section use Iommi's favorite "drop minor third" tuning, where each string is tuned down one and a half steps. The advantage of dropping each string is that all the scale and chord shapes remain unaltered. Everything just sounds deeper and meaner! This example is based around an open C shape (that actually produces a low A chord in this tuning) and is typical of Iommi's work on the Sabbath album *Volume Four*, released in 1972.

Cover art for Black Sabbath's *Volume Four*

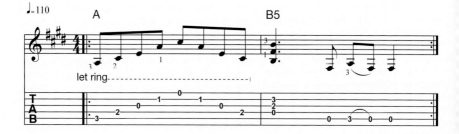

RIFF REGISTER

Function: Huge-sounding opening riff based on a ringing open C chord shape.

Technique: The C-shape chord should be played using alternate picking, ensuring that all the notes are allowed to ring to the end of the bar.

EDCAG position: Shape 3 (open) C shape, followed by shape 2 (open) D shape.

Harmonic content: Uses the diatonic chords bVI (A), bVII (B) and I (C#m) from the natural minor (aeolian mode).

WATCH OUT FOR
FRETTING THE C SHAPE CLEANLY TO ENSURE THAT THE OPEN FIRST AND THIRD STRINGS ARE ALLOWED TO RING CLEARLY.

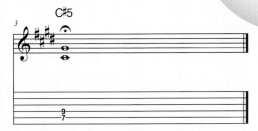

C#5

RIFF NO. 3:
USING THE TRITONE

During the Middle Ages, the tritone (or diminished fifth) interval was known as the *diabolus in musica*—the devil in music—and generally outlawed. If musicians played this dissonant sound it was believed that Satan himself was summoned—so it's no coincidence that the blues, which is littered with tritones, is sometimes known as "the devil's music." Iommi knew how powerful and evocative this interval was, and he incorporated it in many classic Black Sabbath riffs.

Cover of Black Sabbath's 1975 release, *Sabotage*

RIFF REGISTER

Function: Fast, driving main riff punctuated with two-note power chords.

Technique: Although this riff is played at a brisk tempo, using down-picks throughout will create a more menacing sound.

EDCAG position: Uses shape 1 two-note power chords throughout.

Harmonic content: The G5 power chord is built on the diminished fifth of the C# minor scale. By sounding the high C#5 chord immediately after it a "double" tritone is sounded, since the chords are a parallel diminished fifth apart.

WATCH OUT FOR

THE SWIFTLY MOVING POWER CHORDS IN THE FOURTH BAR. PICK THE G5 CHORDS ONLY, SLIDING DOWN (TO F#5) OR UP (TO A5) AS REQUIRED.

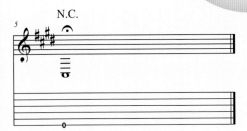

RIFF NO. 4:
SINGLE-NOTE-STYLE

Although many of Iommi's most famous compositions are based around moving power chord shapes, he also penned memorable single-note riffs. These single-note ideas were usually pentatonic-based, but they frequently added notes from the natural minor of the blues scale to facilitate chromatic movement and trills, as here. Most of Iommi's riffs were double-tracked and panned hard right and left to create a bigger sound. On later albums, harmony guitar parts were also overdubbed.

Black Sabbath group shot, 1970

RIFF REGISTER

Function: Two-bar riff used as the basis for an instrumental section in a heavy rock composition.

Technique: Rhythmically accurate slurring technique is required.

EDCAG position: Shape 3 E blues scale with major second (D#) added from natural minor (aeolian mode).

Harmonic content: The heavy blues-based style of this riff is given a characteristic Iommi twist at the end of bar 2 with the trill on the D#. This gives the riff a typical neo-classical flavor.

WATCH OUT FOR

THE QUICK CHANGE FROM FOURTH POSITION (FOR THE TRILL AT THE END OF BAR 2) BACK TO FIFTH POSITION FOR THE REPEAT OF THE RIFF. TRY USING YOUR SECOND AND FOURTH FINGERS FOR THE FIRST THREE NOTES WHEN REPEATING.

EXAMPLE NO. 1:
OPEN G CHORD SHAPES

In the 1960s, Rolling Stones guitarist Keith Richards began experimenting with open tunings. Many of the Stones' iconic riffs were recorded in open G tuning, most famously "Honky Tonk Women" and "Brown Sugar." Don Everly, of the Everly Brothers, also used open G tuning but with the sixth string removed—creating a more concise sound without the low sixth string. Richards adopted Everly's style in the late 1960s and described the resulting freedom as a "musical rebirth."

Mick Jagger and Keith Richards in 1969

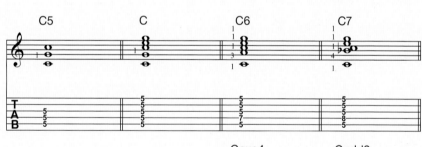

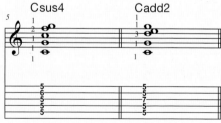

RIFF REGISTER

Function: Open G tuning chord shapes that allow a major chord to be played by barring across any fret with one finger.

Technique: By leaving the first finger barre on the fret, additional notes can be added or substituted with the second and third fingers.

EDCAG position: Shape 4 open G tuning major chord plus variations.

Harmonic content: Adding suspensions such as the major second and perfect fourth or superimposing the triad a perfect fourth above (F/C) becomes much simpler in this tuning.

WATCH OUT FOR

UNLESS YOU'RE GOING TO REMOVE YOUR SIXTH STRING LIKE KEITH RICHARDS, USE THE TIP OF YOUR FIRST FINGER TO PREVENT IT FROM RINGING.

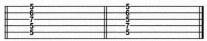

EXAMPLE NO. 2:

ROCK & ROLL BOOGIE-STYLE

Chuck Berry was a big influence on the rhythm style of Keith Richards. In open tuning, that famous chugging de-da-de-da-de-da-de-da rock n' roll riff is not only easier to play, it sounds bigger because you can add the notes of a major chord above it. There are many Stones tracks that feature the open tuning variant of this Berry-esque riff, and Richards still employs it in the recent Stones repertoire where he practices the "ancient art of weaving" with fellow Stones guitarist Ronnie Wood.

Made in the Shade (1975) was The Rolling Stones' first official compilation album

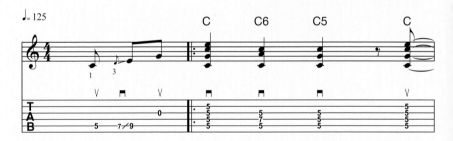

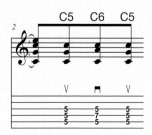

RIFF REGISTER

Function: Two-bar chord-based riff typically used as a verse accompaniment.

Technique: Use alternate eighth-note picking throughout as indicated.

EDCAG position: Shape 4 C major chord (open G shape) with added major 6 (A) and minor seventh (Bb).

Harmonic content: Expands the tonality of the original rock & roll riff (which is based on a two-note power chord) to include the major third.

WATCH OUT FOR

KEEPING THAT SIXTH STRING SILENT BY TOUCHING IT WITH THE TIP OF YOUR FIRST FINGER.

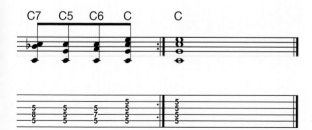

EXAMPLE NO. 3:

THE CLASSIC STONES' F/C CHORD

As we discovered on pages 158–9, creating that illusive suspended sound of the superimposed triad is awkward in normal tuning. In open G tuning these wonderfully ambiguous chord voicings are straightforward, and that Stones rhythm sound is right under your fingertips. The C/G chord in the first bar of this riff is simply the F/C shape moved up to the twelfth fret. That's the joy of this—just moving a chord shape around the neck produces great riffs.

Keith Richards takes time out from recording in Denmark, 1970

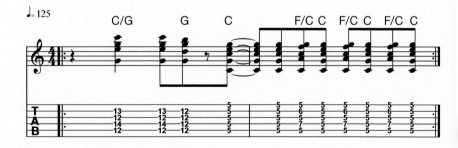

RIFF REGISTER

Function: Two-bar riff that works well as an intro.

Technique: As in the previous example, it's essential to use alternate eighth-note strumming to create a fluid, grooving riff.

EDCAG position: Shape 4 major shape (open G tuning).

Harmonic content: Superimposing a triad a perfect fourth above a root note creates an inversion. The C/G and F/C are simply second inversion (i.e. with the fifth in the bass) variations of C and F.

WATCH OUT FOR

SIMULTANEOUSLY FRETTING WITH YOUR SECOND AND THIRD FINGERS WHILE SUSTAINING THE PRESSURE OF THE FIRST FINGER BARRE.

EXAMPLE NO. 4:
INCORPORATING THE "SUS 2&4" CHORD

When the abbreviation "sus" is included in a chord symbol it means that a "suspended" third should be played. Traditionally, the major second or perfect fourth replace the major third to create the suspension, so sus2 and sus4 symbols are frequent. These chords have long been a part of rock & roll rhythm guitar playing and were first used during the 1950s. In late recordings, Keith Richards took the concept a step further and added the second and fourth simultaneously, creating his own version of the "sus" chord.

Keith Richards and Ronnie Wood rock out on their Bigger Bang tour in 2006

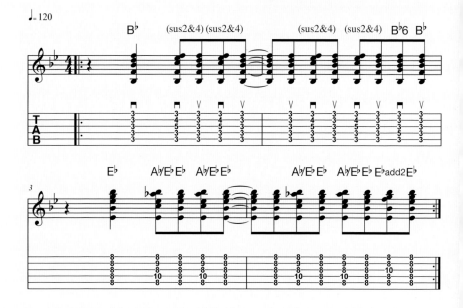

RIFF REGISTER

Function: Four-bar riff perfect for creating a powerful verse accompaniment.

Technique: Use alternate eighth-note strumming throughout keeping the strumming motion constant on rests and longer notes by "ghosting" across the strings with your pick.

EDCAG position: Shape 4 major chord (open G tuning) with suspensions added.

Harmonic content: A classic I (Bb) to IV (Eb) chord sequence. The chord suspensions are achieved with a superimposed triad in bars 3 and 4—so that the note C is regularly sounded throughout the riff.

WATCH OUT FOR

NOT PLAYING ON THE FIRST BEAT OF BARS 1 AND 3. KEEP YOUR STRUMMING ARM MOVING (AS DESCRIBED ABOVE) BUT WITHOUT HITTING THE STRINGS.

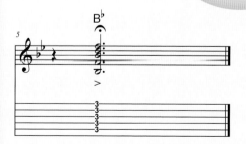

RIFF NO. 1:
THE IRON MAIDEN GALLOP

The Number Of The Beast (1982) was Iron Maiden's third album. It established the band as the front-runners in the new wave of metal groups who were engineering the rebirth of heavy rock. The album was the first to feature their new vocalist Bruce Dickinson, and to the majority of fans, it encapsulates the classic Maiden line-up. The album showcased a confident new sound, which included the iconic "Iron Maiden gallop"–created by playing power chord riffs with sixteenth-note picking pattern.

Adrian Smith performs with Iron Maiden in Madison Square Garden, 1982

1980S METAL RIFFS

RIFF REGISTER

Function: Up-tempo, four-bar power chord riff that would typically be used as a verse or bridge sequence.

Technique: Fast, accurate, alternate sixteenth-note picking is crucial to achieving that trademark "gallop" sound.

EDCAG position: Shape 4, two-note power chords.

Harmonic content: Simple I (D5)–IV (G5) chord sequence is contrasted with a bVII (C5) followed by a first inversion IV (G/B) chord in bar 4.

WATCH OUT FOR
BUILDING UP THE SPEED OF YOUR GALLOP PICKING TECHNIQUE SLOWLY TO ENSURE THE PICKING IS EVEN AND ACCURATE.

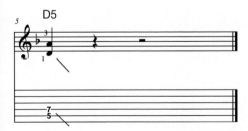

RIFF NO. 2:
BLUESY DOUBLE-STOP RIFFS

Whitesnake found success with a new generation of
musicians who were re-establishing the popularity
of heavy rock in the late 1970s. Vocalist David
Coverdale had already tasted stardom as Deep
Purple's vocalist, and guitarist Bernie Marsden had
found success in the supergroup Paice, Ashton &
Lord. Whitesnake's rock & roll pedigree set them
apart from their peers. They saw that the days of the
extended guitar solo were over, and catchy pop-style
choruses were back. This bluesy, heavy riff is typical
of Whitesnake's hard-hitting early 1980s style.

David Coverdale on tour with Whitesnake in 1982

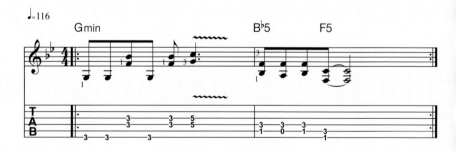

RIFF REGISTER

Function: Two-bar main riff used as a song opener and verse accompaniment.

Technique: Since both the low G notes and the double stops in the first bar are played with the first finger, finger rolling and careful damping should be employed.

EDCAG position: Shape 1 minor pentatonic based riff, followed by shape 4 (Bb5) and shape one (F) power chords.

Harmonic content: Old-school pentatonic double-stop style riff firmly establishes the G minor tonality in the first bar.

WATCH OUT FOR

ENSURE THAT YOUR THIRD FINGER REMAINS FRETTED ON THE FOURTH STRING AS YOU PLAY THE OPEN A IN THE SECOND BAR.

RIFF NO. 3:
1980S ROCK BALLAD-STYLE

Producer Robert John "Mutt" Lange singlehandedly defined the sound of the quintessential 1980s rock ballad. He produced an endless stream of artists from Def Leppard to Bryan Adams. Big, fat, double-tracked processed guitars, huge drums, and ultra-slick arrangements were his forté. Complete with soaring vocals that usually lamented a long lost love, the ballads of the 1980s replaced in-your-face guitar sounds with intricate, heavily chorused arpeggios and sweeping synth pads.

Def Leppard in 1980

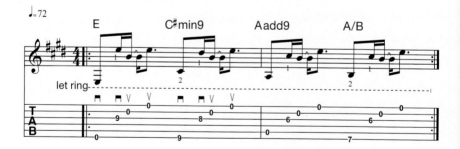

RIFF REGISTER

Function: Two-bar arpeggio riff that would typically feature as an introduction and verse accompaniment.

Technique: Use alternate sixteenth-note picking as indicated. Although this riff could also be played finger-style, it sounds more effective when played with a pick.

EDCAG position: Shape 4 (E), shape 5 (C#min9, A/B), and shape 1 (Aadd9) partial chord shapes are picked against open strings.

Harmonic content: The open E and B notes are restated in each chord against the fretted third string note. This gives a cohesive, hypnotic quality to the riff.

WATCH OUT FOR

NAILING THAT REPEATED, SYNCOPATED SIXTEENTH RHYTHM ACCURATELY. TRY CLAPPING THE RHYTHM ALONG WITH THE CD BEFORE YOU PLAY.

E

RIFF NO. 4:

THRASH METAL-STYLE

Metallica were pioneers of the new thrash metal sound that emerged in the mid 1980s. Scooped mids (achieved by turning the "middle" tone control way down on your amp), blazing tempos, palm-muted riffs, and quirky, non-diatonic chord progressions are all essential thrash metal prerequisites. All these characteristics were present in Metallica's third album, *Master Of Puppets* (1986).

Metallica, in 1985, were already playing to crowds of 60,000

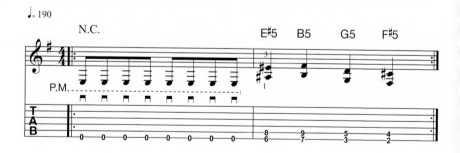

RIFF REGISTER

Function: Two-bar main riff that works most effectively in a verse sequence.

Technique: Unusually at such a fast tempo, downstrokes should be used throughout to enhance the robotic, driving groove.

EDCAG position: Shape 1 moveable power chord shape.

Harmonic content: The power chord sequence in the second bar is based on the blues scale. Moving directly from the open E pedal note to the A#5 creates the tritone interval that is crucial to creating metal sounds.

WATCH OUT FOR

PICKING WITH DOWNPICKS THROUGHOUT AT THIS TEMPO. ALWAYS START BY PRACTICING SLOWLY—IT CAN TAKE WEEKS FOR DEMANDING TECHNIQUES TO START FEELING COMFORTABLE.

LICK NO. 1:

PLAYING CHORDS OVER A BASS PEDAL

When Eddie Van Halen appeared on the music scene in the late 1970s, he made the same impact as Jimi Hendrix had a decade earlier—he turned the guitar world upside down. Nobody had heard guitar pyrotechnics on this scale before: whammy bar dive bombs, frenzied tremolo picking, and two-handed tapping which created impossible flurries of notes. Like Hendrix before him, this virtuoso musician spawned legions of clones, but few touched the originality and musicality of Eddie Van Halen.

Eddie Van Halen popularized the "tapping" technique in the 1970s (see page 176)

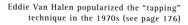

EDDIE VAN HALEN - STYLE

RIFF REGISTER

Function: Two-bar intro riff that establishes a solid groove before settling into a simpler verse accompaniment.

Technique: Accurate barring and picking is required to ensure only the tabbed notes of the chord are sounded.

EDCAG position: Second inversion (fifth as lowest note) shape 4 major triads with shape 4 power chords.

Harmonic content: By sustaining the D5 chord over the constant E bass note, an E11 (D/E) chord is created, introducing mixolydian color tones such as the minor seventh (D) and major ninth (F#).

WATCH OUT FOR

CREATING THE PERCUSSIVE OPENING NOTES BY BARRING OVER THE EIGHTH FRET (BARRING OVER THE NINTH WILL CREATE UNWANTED HARMONICS).

LICK NO. 2:

TWO-HANDED TAPPING-STYLE

Two-handed tapping creates stunning effects in the hands of a skilled player. When poorly applied it just ends up sounding like a mess of notes with no connection with the chord sequence. Avoid this by considering the harmony you're playing the lick over, and concentrating on exactly how you're subdividing each beat. If your first finger is tapping regularly against the pulse then you can decide whether to hammer-on groups of two, three, or four notes with your fretting-hand fingers.

Eddie Van Halen in 1982

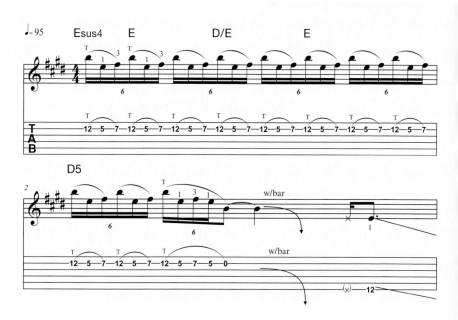

EDDIE VAN HALEN-STYLE

RIFF REGISTER

Function: Static tapping lick (i.e., it remains on the same six-note pattern) that works well as a solo ending phrase.

Technique: By tapping your index finger onto the second string at the twelfth fret a high B is generated. Releasing the finger with a flicking motion achieves a lower, fretted note.

EDCAG position: Shape 3 major pentatonic with the high tapped note generated from the shape 1 major pentatonic.

Harmonic content: Because the major third is not included in the lick, this tapping phrase will happily fit over all of the chords in the sequence.

WATCH OUT FOR

MAKE SURE YOUR LEFT HAND IS IN POSITION AND THE LOWER NOTE IS FRETTED BEFORE YOU BEGIN THE TAPPING LICK.

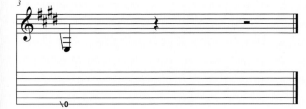

LICK NO. 3:
SOUNDING OPEN STRINGS AGAINST FRETTED NOTES

Eddie Van Halen's riffs were just as exciting as his high-octane solos. What's also interesting is the sound he used to play them, shunning the processed guitar sound of the late 1970s and early 1980s with its thick chorusing and heavy compression. This gives his earlier recordings a gutsy, timeless quality, making them sound as fresh today as they did three decades ago. He was also never afraid to incorporate clichés, such as the simple quarter-tone bends played against the A5 chord in this example.

Van Halen (1978) has sold over ten million copies in the USA alone

RIFF REGISTER

Function: Two-bar riff that functions as an opening sequence, or in a verse section, when underplaying (i.e., leaving out some of the notes) and softer picking would be used.

Technique: Alternate eighth-note picking should be used throughout.

EDCAG position: Shape 4 (open) power chord and shape 3 D triad (with open G replacing the fifth).

Harmonic content: An A5 rock & roll lick is contrasted against a Dadd4 chord. By sounding the latter against a constant A bass pedal note, harmonic ambiguity is created.

WATCH OUT FOR

ALLOWING THE DADD4/A CHORD TO RING FOR AS LONG AS POSSIBLE BEFORE YOU CHANGE POSITION TO PLAY THE DESCENDING CHROMATIC LINE.

EDDIE VAN HALEN - STYLE

LICK NO. 4:
TREMOLO PICKING-STYLE

Ask any guitar player what is the main feature of Eddie Van Halen's lead work and they'll start talking about two-handed tapping. Although many of his solos feature the technique, there are also plenty of solos that use tremolo picking, bends, wide vibrato, and whammy bar dive bombs to create equally dazzling bursts of virtuosity. This lick attempts to demonstrate the advanced picking-hand technique that was evident even on the earliest Van Halen recordings.

This style was one of Van Halen's most famous riffs in the late 1970s

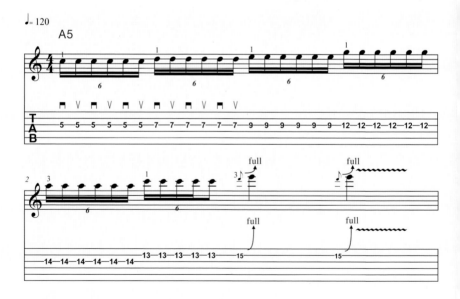

EDDIE VAN HALEN - STYLE

RIFF REGISTER

Function: Lick that stretches over three bars. Works well as a climactic solo ending.

Technique: Alternate picking should be applied, using small movements and angling the pick slightly across the string to facilitate faster picking.

EDCAG position: Ascending phrase that begins in shape 1 A minor pentatonic and climbs the third string until it reaches shape 4.

Harmonic content: All of the notes used belong to the A minor pentatonic, proving that you don't need exotic scales to create flashy licks!

WATCH OUT FOR

ALWAYS PRACTICE DEMANDING TECHNICAL EXERCISES SLOWLY, USING A METRONOME AND INCREASING TEMPO VERY GRADUALLY (OVER DAYS OR EVEN WEEKS).

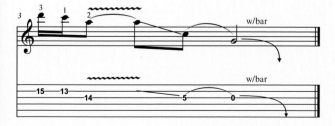

RIFF NO. 1:
BOSTON-STYLE RIFF

Boston were the original stadium rockers. Their 1976 self-titled album was one of the biggest-selling debut albums in American history, and songs from the recording remain high on the airplay lists of classic rock radio stations to this day. They established themselves as one of the biggest stadium attractions in the United States. Guitarist Tom Scholz was an electronics wizard and designed his own guitar processing units to create the huge, guitar wall-of-sound that became Boston's trademark.

Tom Scholz in New York in 1978

RIFF REGISTER

Function: Barnstorming two-bar riff used as the basis for a chorus section.

Technique: Alternate sixteenth-note strumming should be "ghosted" throughout the riff to ensure the percussive sixteenth-note strums are played fluently.

EDCAG position: Shape 1 and shape 4 three- and four-note power chords. Shape 1 first inversion G (G/B) is also used in the second bar.

Harmonic content: The I (G5)–VI (E5) is a diatonic major chord sequence. By using a power chord as the VI chord, a less minor sound is created.

WATCH OUT FOR

PLAYING ALL THE POWER CHORDS ACCURATELY AND RHYTHMICALLY TO CREATE A SLICK FM RADIO STYLE SOUND.

G5

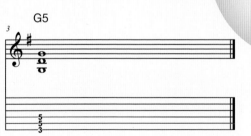

RIFF NO. 2:
AC/DC-STYLE RIFF

Incredibly, AC/DC have been rocking
audiences for over 35 years. Their no-
nonsense, no-frills brand of rock & roll
has never gone out of fashion—as over
200 million worldwide album sales testify.
Although their album *Black Ice* (2008), was
their first since 2000, it took just one week to
reach the number 1 slot in the Billboard Hard
Rock Chart. The band have toured the world
many times over, so they know a thing or two
about getting an audience on its feet.

Angus Young's riffs may seem austere by some standards,
but they are perfect for AC/DC's inimitable style

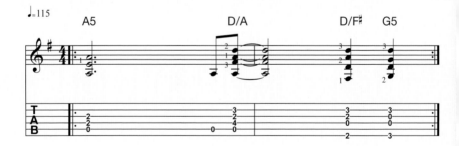

RIFF REGISTER

Function: Two-bar chorus riff that leaves plenty of space for the vocalist to let rip!

Technique: The only way to really make these riffs sound good is to play them loud! So it's very important to ensure that any unwanted open strings are damped with the fretting-hand fingers.

EDCAG position: Shape 1 and 4 power chords contrasted with shape 3 (D/A) and shape 2 (D/F#) major chords.

Harmonic content: The bass pedal (A) over the first two chords creates interest as the IV (D) becomes an inversion with its fifth in the bass.

WATCH OUT FOR

MAKE SURE YOUR LEFT HAND IS IN POSITION AND THE LOWER NOTE IS FRETTED BEFORE YOU BEGIN THE TAPPING LICK.

A5

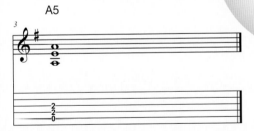

RIFF NO. 3:
BON JOVI "TALK BOX"-STYLE

New Jersey rockers Bon Jovi were one of the hottest stadium-filling acts of the 1980s and remain big crowd-pullers today. The band's third album, *Slippery When Wet* (1986), remains their most commercially successful album. Richie Sambora used a talk box on the album to create the riff for "Livin' On A Prayer," which has become the band's signature song. The talk box sends the guitar's signal through a tube into the guitarist's mouth; and produces unusual sounds.

Bon Jovi performing in
New York (1980)

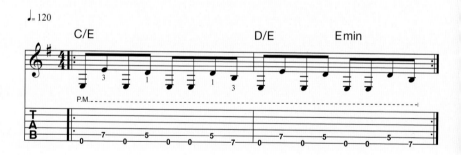

RIFF REGISTER

Function: Two-bar riff used as the intro and main theme of anthemic rock song.

Technique: When played with a voice box, the mouth should be opened wide to change the sound on the off-beat of beats 1, 2, and 4. Naturally, this will take some practice!

EDCAG position: Shape 3 E minor pentatonic-based riff with added low open E string.

Harmonic content: Although this a straightforward E minor pentatonic riff, the triads played on the keyboard create tension resolved on the E minor chord in the second bar.

WATCH OUT FOR

USING THAT TALK BOX—YOU'LL DISCOVER THAT IT'S A BIT LIKE TRYING TO SIMULTANEOUSLY TAP YOUR HEAD AND RUB YOUR STOMACH!

Fmin

RIFF NO. 4:
U2-STYLE WITH DELAY

The first stadium gig to be televised worldwide was Live Aid back in 1985. U2 established themselves as a world-class act after their performance at this monumental event. Now a world-class star, guitarist The Edge created his signature sound by using echo effects to create huge riffs from a handful of arpeggio notes. The repeats sound against successive notes and create a rhythmic cascading effect that has become an integral part of the U2 sound.

The Edge performs at Live 8 in 2005

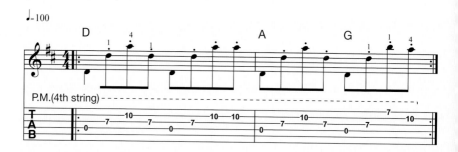

STADIUM ROCK RIFFS

RIFF REGISTER

Function: Two-bar arpeggio-based riff that functions as the main theme in a pop-rock song.

Technique: Many echo/delay effects units now have a "tap tempo" function. Set the feedback level to around 50% and the wet/dry mix the same. A 350ms setting provides the correct length of delay.

EDCAG position: Shape 5 D5 arpeggio with high B added in the second bar.

Harmonic content: Sounding the basic D5 arpeggio against the changing chords transforms the A chord to A add4 and the G add9, making a basic I–V–IV sequence far more interesting.

WATCH OUT FOR

DAMPING THE FOURTH STRING WITH YOUR PICKING HAND AND KEEPING THE UPPER NOTES SHORT BY RELEASING THE PRESSURE OF YOUR FRETTING-HAND FINGERS.

RIFF NO. 1:
R.E.M.-STYLE

R.E.M. spearheaded the 1980s alternative rock movement. They embraced the style of 1960s garage bands: quirky melodies and infectious riffs. R.E.M. were the antithesis of the shred metal music of the day. It was not until the release of *Out of Time* and *Automatic for the People* in the early 1990s that they were finally rewarded with mainstream success. Guitarist Peter Buck creates his trademark sound by blending chords with open strings and arpeggios.

Peter Buck at the Longest Day festival, Milton Keynes, UK, 1985

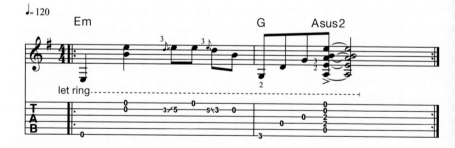

RIFF REGISTER

Function: Two-bar, chord-based riff used as an intro and chorus accompaniment.

Technique: Use alternate eighth-note picking throughout to ensure the riff sounds rhythmical and fluid.

EDCAG position: Shape 1 (Em), 5 (G), and 4 (Asus2) chords.

Harmonic content: By omitting the third of each chord in the sequence, this open chord-based riff manages to sound edgy and cool.

WATCH OUT FOR
INADVERTENTLY MUTING AN OPEN STRING NEXT TO A FRETTED NOTE. AIM TO KEEP YOUR FINGERS AT 90 DEGREES TO AVOID TOUCHING THE OPEN STRINGS (PARTICULARLY AT THE END OF THE FIRST BAR).

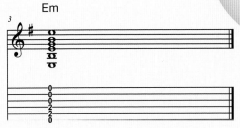

Em

RIFF NO. 2:
RADIOHEAD-STYLE

Radiohead are the British champions of alternative rock. Their first single, "Creep" (1992), was a massive success which they only eclipsed with the release of *The Bends* in 1995. This recording showcased the band's skilled songwriting and established their trademark sound: quirky chord sequences delivered with intelligent, multilayered guitar parts. Lead guitarist Jonny Greenwood frequently uses octaves to create dramatic, climbing lines.

Thom Yorke and Jonny Greenwood at London's Hammersmith Apollo, 2006

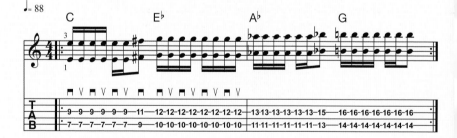

ALTERNATIVE ROCK RIFFS

RIFF REGISTER

Function: Two-bar intro; also an ending for chorus sequences.

Technique: Octaves fretted with the first and third fingers and played with alternate sixteenth-note strumming. Adjacent open strings must be damped with the fretting-hand fingers to prevent them from sounding.

EDCAG position: Octave shape with lowest note on the fifth string.

Harmonic content: A climbing riff is created by focusing on the major third of each chord in the sequence. Because the chord progression is non-diatonic, the thirds never sound too "sugary" as they might in a more conventional sequence.

WATCH OUT FOR
STRUMMING EVENLY AND RHYTHMICALLY TO CREATE A STRONG OCTAVE LINE. MAKE SURE ALL OPEN STRINGS ARE DAMPED.

RIFF NO. 3:

FOO FIGHTERS-STYLE

The Foo Fighters were formed by Dave
Grohl after the dissolution of Nirvana.
Switching from drums to guitar and
vocal, he wrote the band's debut album
singlehandedly. Grohl's drummer's
perspective is clearly evident in his
guitar riffs, which often feature unusual
note groupings and time signatures.
These always sound very natural, never
overblown or self-congratulatory as they
might in a prog rock or fusion context.

Dave Grohl performing in Holland, 2008

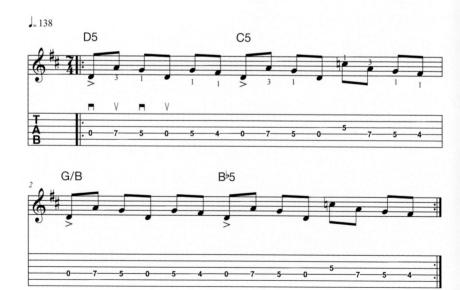

RIFF REGISTER

Function: Main riff that provides an instrumental interlude after each chorus section.

Technique: Alternate eighth-note picking is crucial for creating a relaxed, grooving riff.

EDCAG position: Shape 4 D mixolydian mode.

Harmonic content: Although this riff is written with a D major key signature, it has more in common with a D minor chord sequence. The addition of the C natural in the riff further enhances the riff's harmonic ambiguity.

WATCH OUT FOR

TRYING TO COUNT UP TO SEVEN! MUSICIANS TEND TO COUNT ODD METERS AS GROUPS OF NOTES. IN THIS INSTANCE THE GROUPING IS 3 + 4 SO YOU COUNT: "1, 2, 3" + "1, 2, 3, 4."

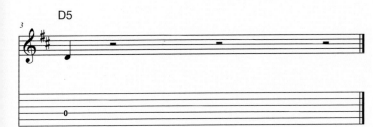

D5

RIFF NO. 4:
RAGE AGAINST THE MACHINE-STYLE

Although not as commercially successful as some alternative rock groups, rap rock bands enjoyed high cult status in the 1990s. Rage Against the Machine guitarist Tom Morello uses drop-D tuning to create deep and mean bluesy riffs. Drop-D, as its name suggests, involves dropping the sixth string (low E) down a step to D. One advantage of this is that power chords can be created by barring across the lower strings with one finger, making them almost as easy to play as single notes.

Tom Morello performing at the
Leeds Festival, UK, 2008

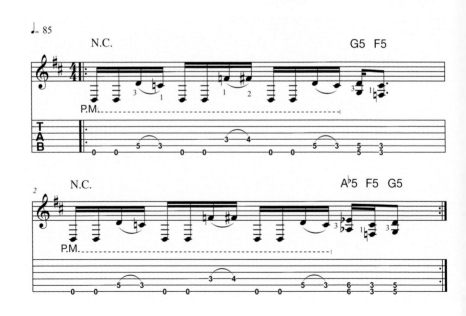

RIFF REGISTER

Function: Main riff and verse riff in a rap rock arrangement. In a verse setting the riff would be completely palm muted and picked softer.

Technique: Alternate sixteenth-note picking with accurate string jumping required to move between open sixth string and higher notes. Palm muting to be applied to sixth string only.

EDCAG position: Shape 3 D blues scale with added major third (F#).

Harmonic content: Although Rage Against the Machine's riffs sounded aggressive at the time, hindsight reveals the heavy blues influence apparent in Morello's earlier work.

WATCH OUT FOR

REMEMBERING TO DROP YOUR SIXTH STRING DOWN A TONE! THE NOTE ON THE SEVENTH FRET SHOULD SOUND THE SAME AS THE OPEN FIFTH STRING WHEN YOU'RE IN TUNE.

D5

RIFF NO. 1:
STANDARD TUNING RIFF

Despite its humble beginnings as a Seattle-based underground movement, grunge made a big impact on the 1990s music scene. Nirvana's career was cut short by the death of frontman Kurt Cobain in 1994. Although the band released only three albums, they are regarded as one of the most important and influential bands of the 1990s. Cobain experimented with different tunings throughout the band's career, but also recorded in standard tuning, as in this example.

Kurt Cobain recording in
Hilversum Studios, Holland, 1991

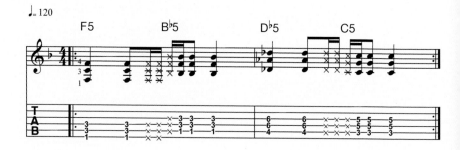

RIFF REGISTER

Function: Two-bar power chord riff that functions as an intro and chorus accompaniment.

Technique: Muted chords add a percussive quality to this already driving riff. This is achieved by just releasing the pressure of your fretting fingers without removing them from the strings.

EDCAG position: Shape 1 and shape 4 three-note power chords.

Harmonic content: Although written in F major, the use of power chords (with no third) and the inclusion of the non-diatonic bVI chord (Db5) create a characteristic, harmonically ambiguous sequence.

WATCH OUT FOR

KEEPING YOUR FRETTING-HAND FINGERS IN CONTACT WITH THE STRINGS WHEN PLAYING THE MUTED NOTES.

F5

RIFF NO. 2:
STANDARD TUNING DOWN A WHOLE STEP

Kurt Cobain frequently tuned his guitar lower without tuning to a chord or dropping the sixth string as many other 1990s rock players did. The tuning used in this example is a whole step lower (low to high: D–G–C–F–A–D), so hitting an open E shape produces a low, dark-sounding D chord. The effect you can hear on the recording is a chorus pedal; Cobain used an Electro-Harmonix Small Clone pedal to produce that lush, warbling sound.

Nirvana in Frankfurt, Germany, 1991

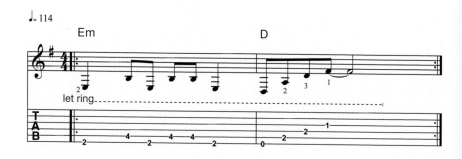

200

RIFF REGISTER

Function: Intro riff that also functions as a verse accompaniment. The subtle arpeggios providing a stark contrast to a thrash-style chorus.

Technique: Double stop (Em) and chord shape (D) picked with alternate eighth-note picking.

EDCAG position: Shape 5 double stop (Em) and shape 1 open chord (D).

Harmonic content: The low root note and minor third of the E minor chord create a dark, eerie soundscape when allowed to ring into each other. The simple open E chord shape produces a much lower, darker D major chord in this tuning.

WATCH OUT FOR

ALLOWING THE OPENING NOTES TO SUSTAIN INTO EACH OTHER—JUST LIKE PICKING THE NOTES OUT OF AN OPEN CHORD.

RIFF NO. 3:
DROP-D TUNING-STYLE

Drop-D tunings were originally used by blues and fingerstyle folk guitarists. They were adopted in the 1980s by the new wave of rock guitarists, and remained in vogue in the 1990s. One of the main advantages of drop-D tuning is that it allows you to play a three-note power chord with just one finger. Kurt Cobain used drop-D tuning for many Nirvana tunes; it allowed him to create unusual chord progressions just by moving his finger up and down the guitar neck.

Kurt Cobain stagediving at the ManRay nightclub, Cambridge, MA, 1990

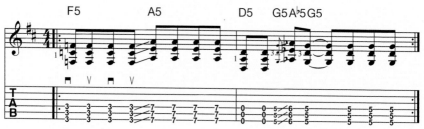

RIFF REGISTER

Function: Low, menacing power chord riff used in grunge-style chorus.

Technique: Many rock players use constant down-picks to create a driving sound. Kurt Cobain wanted to produce a larger, denser sound with his power chords. This is achieved by using alternate eighth-note strumming throughout.

EDCAG position: Shape 1, drop-D power chord shape (barring across the frets with one finger).

Harmonic content: By starting the riff on the non-diatonic bIII (F5) chord, the D major tonality is disguised until bar 2. The chromatic slide in the second bar is based on a D blues scale root movement.

WATCH OUT FOR

USING YOUR THIRD FINGER FOR THE G5 AND A5 CHORDS. THIS MAKES THE RETURN TO F5 ON THE REPEAT MUCH EASIER.

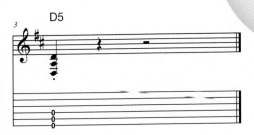

D5

RIFF NO. 4:
DROP-C# TUNING-STYLE

If you want to create darker, meaner-sounding riffs there's only one place to go: down! By taking a regular drop-D tuning and then lowering every string a half step (low to high: C#–G#–C#–F#–A#–D#), the resulting power chords sound even more resonant. Kurt Cobain took Tony Iommi's idea of tuning down to achieve bigger sounds and mixed it with drop-D tuning. Riffs in drop C# tuning can be found on all three of Nirvana's albums.

Cover art for *Bleach*–Nirvana's debut album (1989)

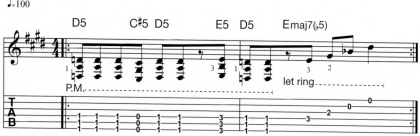

RIFF REGISTER

Function: Two-bar power chord riff that could be used as an instrumental section or vocal accompaniment.

Technique: Palm muting is used to prevent the power chords from ringing, creating a dark, percussive rhythm part.

EDCAG position: Shape 1 drop-D (the same shapes work in drop C#) power chord shapes. Shape 1 major chord (E) with added open strings.

Harmonic content: This sequence is in D minor so the C#5 creates a phrygian (think Spanish guitar) harmonic backdrop, further enhanced by the Emaj7(b5) chord in bar 2.

WATCH OUT FOR

MAKING SURE YOUR PALM IS VERY CLOSE TO THE BRIDGE AND DAMPING ACROSS THE LOWEST THREE STRINGS (NOT JUST THE SIXTH STRING).

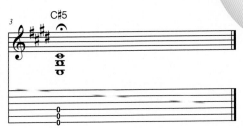

RIFF NO. 1:
BLUR-STYLE

The dominance of American grunge music in the late 1980s and early 1990s prompted a musical reaction in the UK. A new wave of bands emerged, keen to refocus audiences on homegrown talent. They drew their influences from 1960s icons such as The Kinks and The Beatles. Blur were one of the earliest Britpop groups to enjoy success. Their self-titled fifth album (1997) was a success on both sides of the Atlantic. This riff is typical of the material Blur produced in the mid to late 1990s.

Blur in Holborn Studio, London, 1996

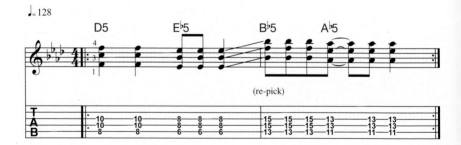

RIFF REGISTER

Function: Heavily distorted two-bar riff that functions as both intro and chorus accompaniment.

Technique: Playing all the chords on the same three strings requires deft sliding around the neck, particularly at the end of the first bar.

EDCAG position: Shape 4 three-note power chords.

Harmonic content: The sequence uses diatonic power chords from F natural minor (aeolian mode). Note that a second, overdubbed guitar, sounds a constant Ab against the sequence which implies the chords: Fmin–Ebsus4–Bb7(no third)–Ab5.

WATCH OUT FOR

KEEPING YOUR FINGERS IN CONTACT WITH THE STRINGS WHEN CHANGING CHORDS— JUST RELEASE THE PRESSURE AND SLIDE YOUR FINGERS ALONG THE STRINGS.

F5

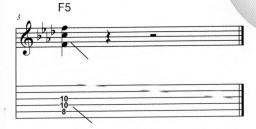

RIFF NO. 2:
PULP-STYLE

Pulp enjoyed a string of hits in the UK, but didn't succeed in exporting their blend of disco, pop, and punk to America—perhaps due to their lyrics' recurring theme of English working-class life. Their album *Different Class* (1996) was a huge success. Outside the UK, the band achieved most fame for maverick frontman Jarvis Cocker's invasion of the 1996 Brit Awards. This riff illustrates how the band fused post-punk flavored riffs with disco grooves to create their iconic sound.

Jarvis Cocker and Steve Mackey
performing live onstage, 1995

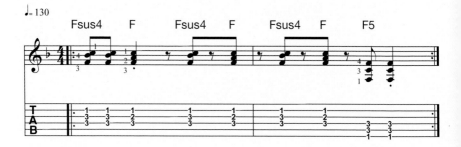

BRITPOP-STYLE RIFFS

RIFF REGISTER

Function: Opening riff that also works well as a verse accompaniment.

Technique: Effective string damping is essential to prevent the chords from ringing and also to avoid sounding adjacent open strings if hit with the pick.

EDCAG position: Shape 1 major and sus4 major shape derived from the full six-string barre chord.

Harmonic content: The simple oscillation between suspended and major tonic chord creates a rhythmic, driving riff.

WATCH OUT FOR

THE QUICK CHANGE TO THE F5 POWER CHORD AT THE END OF THE SECOND BAR— KEEP YOUR FINGERS IN CONTACT WITH THE STRINGS WHILE CHANGING TO PLAY THE REST.

RIFF NO. 3:
OASIS-STYLE

Oasis enjoyed huge sales during the Britpop era. But by the end of the 1990s they seemed to have lost their magic, and sales were waning. The band re-emerged in 2005 with a successful sixth album, *Don't Believe The Truth*. A sell-out world tour and compilation album followed in 2006, which saw the band back at the top of their game. This rhythmic, driving acoustic guitar riff is representative of the band's style on their hit second album, *(What's The Story) Morning Glory?*

Oasis' Noel Gallagher performing live onstage in Amsterdam, 2005

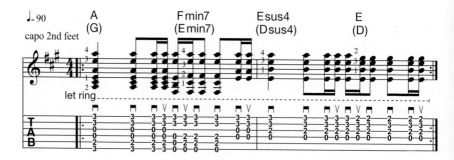

RIFF REGISTER

Function: Main riff; also works well as an unaccompanied opening riff.

Technique: Played with a capo on the second fret to transpose the open chord strum pattern to the key of A major. Use alternate sixteenth-note strumming throughout as indicated.

EDCAG position: Open position chord shapes that all share the same top two notes until the last chord (E).

Harmonic content: By incorporating the high E and A notes into all but the last chord, a cohesive, contemporary accompaniment is created.

WATCH OUT FOR
KEEPING YOUR THIRD AND FOURTH FINGERS FIRMLY IN POSITION ON THE TOP STRINGS WHEN CHANGING CHORDS.

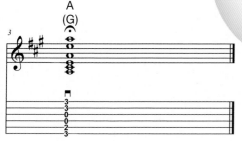

RIFF NO. 4:

SUPERGRASS-STYLE

Supergrass enjoyed huge popularity in the
wake of the Britpop pioneers. And, like all the
other bands featured here, they represented a
return to guitar-based rock & roll—one in the
eye for those who'd declared that the guitar's
dominance in popular music was over by the
start of the 1990s. This riff is representative
of the work on their third album, *Supergrass*
(1999). By this point the band were exploring
more complex instrumentation and moving
away from their post-punk power trio sound.

Supergrass in
Amsterdam, 1999

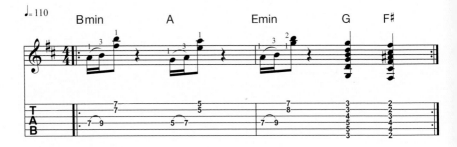

RIFF REGISTER

Function: Double-stop-based riff providing an effective chorus accompaniment that purposely avoids sounding guitar-dominant.

Technique: Use alternate eighth-note picking using downstrokes for the hammer-ons and upstrokes for the double stops.

EDCAG position: Double-stop phrases based on shape 1 and shape 4 chord shapes. Followed by full shape 1 major barre chords.

Harmonic content: B natural minor (aeolian mode) based chord progression; incorporates an F# dominant (with no seventh) by switching to B harmonic minor.

WATCH OUT FOR

KEEPING THOSE HAMMER-ONS RHYTHMICAL—THE DOUBLE STOPS MUST FALL ON THE OFFBEATS.

Bmin

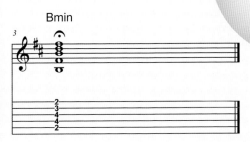

SCALES & CHOPS

SCALE NO. 1:
THE MINOR PENTATONIC

Scale Type: 5-note, minor

Formulae: R–b3–4–5–b7–Oct

Usage: Tonic minor scale that can also be superimposed over dominant and major chords.

Characteristics: Although this is a minor scale, rock musicians have been forcing it over major and dominant seventh chords since the early days of rock & roll—a technique borrowed from the blues pioneers. The minor third and minor seventh are frequently played slightly sharp by applying quarter-tone bends, regardless of what chord type the scale is played over.

Practice Notes: All five shapes for the scale are given here in A minor. The scale should be practiced in all keys. To maximize your fluency in each shape, try moving simple licks from shape one to the remaining four shapes. Root notes have been highlighted in each shape with an "R" between the staves. These "target notes" are essential for creating effective licks.

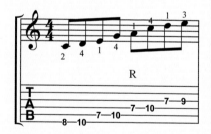

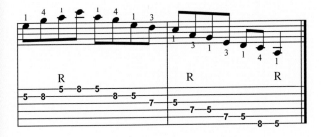

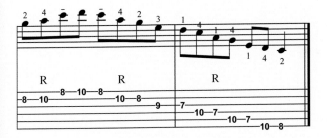

SCALE NO. 1:

THE MINOR PENTATONIC

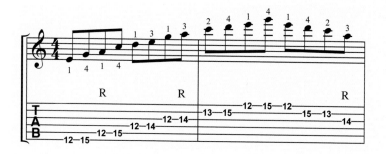

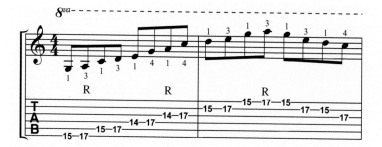

CHOPS BUILDER NO. 1:
MINOR PENTATONIC CHOPS BUILDER

Scale practice is crucial for effective improvisation. But merely whizzing up and down them from the lowest to the highest note won't prepare you for real-world improvising scenarios. You need to get inside them, approaching each note from every possible angle in order to achieve a practical level of fluency. The following exercises are not an exhaustive resource, but they will fast-track your technique and build fingerboard knowledge when practiced regularly.

Practice Notes: These patterns are given in shape 1 only (with the exception of the string bending exercise that climbs the top three strings) and should be applied to the remaining four shapes. Adjacent notes on the same fret should be played with the "finger rolling" technique, i.e. without lifting your finger off the string. Always practice with a metronome and start slowly, only increasing the tempo once total fluency has been achieved. Alternate picking should be religiously applied to the first two examples. Examples 3 and 4, on pages 222–3, can be played with either down-picks or alternate picking; ideally both should be practiced.

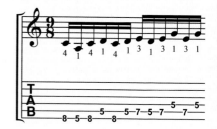

CHOPS BUILDER NO. 1:
MINOR PENTATONIC CHOPS BUILDER

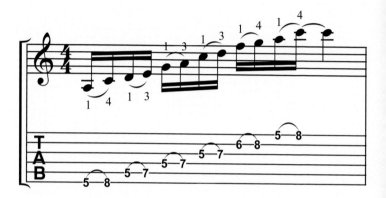

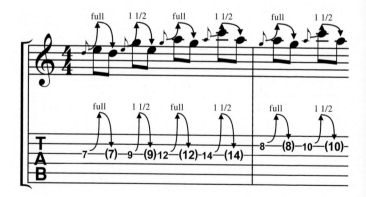

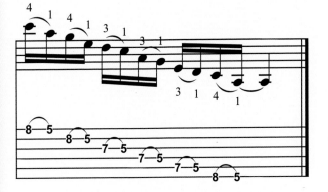

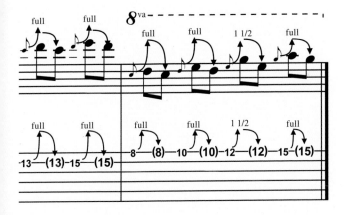

SCALE NO. 2:
THE MAJOR PENTATONIC

Scale Type: 5-note, major

Formulae: R–2–3–5–6–Oct

Usage: Tonic major scale that can be played over major or dominant seventh chords.

Characteristics: This five-note pentatonic scale is the rock guitarists' first choice for soloing in a major key. Since the problematic fourth and seventh of the major scale are omitted, the possibility of playing a "wrong" note is greatly reduced. Also, because there is no seventh in the scale, it can also be used over dominant seventh chords.

Practice Notes: All five shapes for the scale are given here in C major. As with the minor pentatonic, practice the shapes in all keys. To maximize your fluency in each shape, try moving simple licks from shape 1 to the remaining four shapes. Root notes have been highlighted in each shape with an "R" between the staves. These "target notes" are essential for creating effective licks.

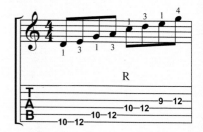

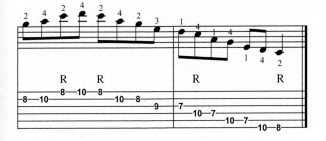

SCALE NO. 2:

THE MAJOR PENTATONIC

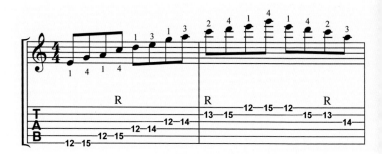

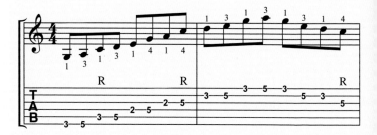

CHOPS BUILDER NO. 2:
MAJOR PENTATONIC CHOPS BUILDER

Because of the close relationship between the major and its relative minor, these shape 1 C major patterns double as shape 2 A minor patterns. By exploiting this relationship you could instantly double your arsenal of licks. For instance, a cool-sounding A minor shape 1 lick can also be played over C major–you'll just be playing in shape 5 C major pentatonic instead. However, you should be aware of the shifting note emphasis. Just compare the "R" symbols of example 1 C major pentatonic with example 2 of the A minor pentatonic shapes. Same notes in the scale, but the root notes (and consequently all the other chord tones) fall in different places–you'll need to be aware of this when you're improvising.

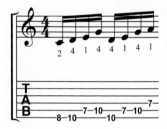

Practice Notes: As with the minor pentatonic, these major pentatonic patterns should be practiced in all five shapes. In example 3, keep the lowest note fretted when playing the hammer-ons; the second note is created by bringing your finger firmly and quickly onto the higher fret. Similarly, pull-offs are played by flicking your finger sideways as you release it. Remember that only regular, repeated practice will yield the best results–why not keep a practice journal so that you can keep a track of when and what you practice?

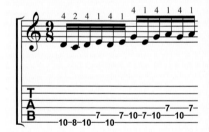

CHOPS BUILDER NO. 2:

MAJOR PENTATONIC CHOPS BUILDER

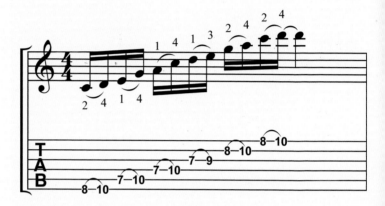

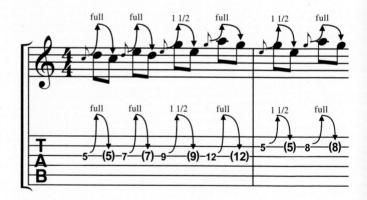

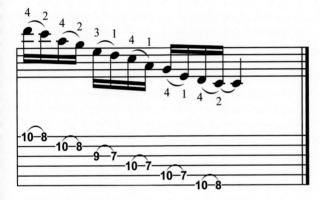

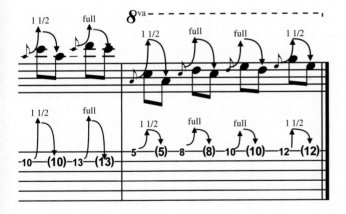

SCALE NO. 3:
THE MAJOR SCALE

Scale Type: 7-note, major

Formulae: R–2–3–4–5–6–7–Oct

Usage: The major scale is not only perfect for generating riffs and licks over major chords, but is also used to generate the major modes commonly used for improvising.

Characteristics: A very "inside"-sounding scale that adds the perfect fourth and major seventh to the major pentatonic. Both these notes should be handled with care and, unless you're playing over a jazzy major seventh chord, both notes should be used as passing notes (i.e., lingering on them can create unwanted dissonance).

Practice Notes: Because this scale is achieved by adding two notes to the major pentatonic, the two scales should be practiced together. Start with shape 1 major pentatonic followed by the shape 1 major scale, moving through all five shapes in the same way. Once you're confident in the key of C, the patterns should be transposed to other keys (beginning with G, F, A, and E). Alternate picking should be used for each shape, taking care to preserve the picking pattern when changing strings. As before, root notes have been highlighted in each shape with an "R" between the staves.

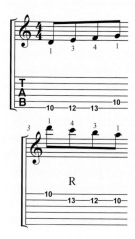

SCALE NO. 3:

THE MAJOR SCALE

CHOPS BUILDER NO. 3:
MAJOR SCALE CHOPS BUILDER

Although the major pentatonic is fine for soloing in a major key, the full 7-note major scale should also be an essential weapon in your improvising arsenal. The scale adds just two notes to the major pentatonic, but it's these two notes that give the major scale its greater melodic potential. Shredders prefer the major scale because it provides those all-important three-notes-per-string patterns—perfect for legato phrasing.

Practice Notes: It's essential that you transfer these ideas to the remaining four shapes of the CAGED system. Once you can play the ideas fluently in all five shapes, transferring them to other keys will be easy. In this way you are simultaneously expanding both your harmonic and fingerboard knowledge. Example 1 is a great vehicle for practicing finger rolling—simply flatten your finger to play the adjacent fret without taking it off the string. In Example 2, follow the fingering indicated and use alternate picking throughout. Example 3 is a three-notes-per-string slurring exercise so its perfect for developing a slick legato technique—pick only the first note on each string and practice it ascending and descending. Finally, Example 4 starts on the fifth fret and climbs two octaves, using a half-step bend to hit the final high C. Bend each note with your third finger, placing your first and second fingers behind it for increased strength.

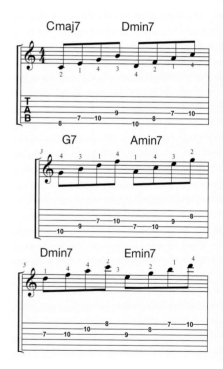

Emin7   **Fmaj7**

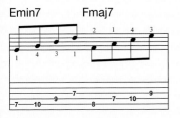

Bmin7b5   **Cmaj7**

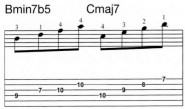

Amin7   **Cmaj7**
                              etc

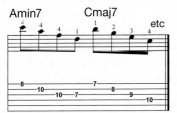

CHOPS BUILDER NO. 3:

MAJOR SCALE CHOPS BUILDER

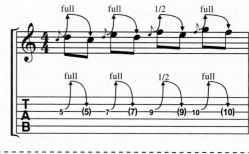

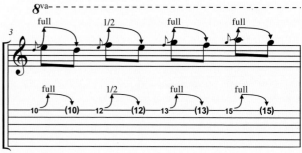

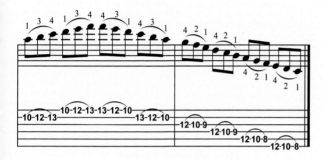

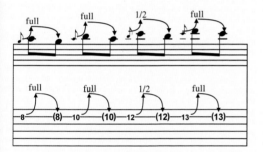

SCALE NO. 4:
THE AEOLIAN MODE

Scale Type: 7-note, minor

Formulae: R–2–b3–4–5–b6–b7–Oct

Usage: The aeolian mode adds two color tones to the minor pentatonic: the major second and minor sixth. It's perfect for generating three-notes-per-string legato licks and for adding neo-classical trills to minor key solos.

Characteristics: The aeolian mode is also known as the "natural" minor scale because it contains the same notes as its relative major cousin. There are four primary minor scales—aeolian and dorian modes plus harmonic and melodic minor scales. Most guitarists learn the aeolian mode first. The only notes that differ between these minor scales are the sixth and/or seventh interval: e.g., in the aeolian the sixth is minor, while in the dorian it's major. Once you've mastered these shapes you can generate other scales by altering the sixth and/or seventh degrees of the aeolian mode.

Practice Notes: It's a good idea to practice the minor pentatonic and aeolian mode together. Start with the shape 1 minor pentatonic followed by the shape 1 aeolian mode, moving through all five shapes in this way. Once you're confident in the key of A minor, the patterns should be transposed to other keys (starting with D, E, B, and G minor). Alternate picking should be used for each shape, taking care to preserve the picking pattern when changing strings.

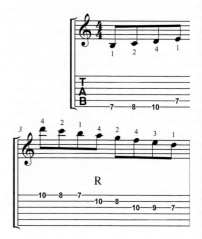

SCALE NO. 4:

THE AEOLIAN MODE

243

CHOPS BUILDER NO. 4:
AEOLIAN MODE CHOPS BUILDER

There's no doubt that the minor pentatonic is great for soloing in minor keys. The aeolian mode takes things a step further, adding more colors and a touch of class to your minor key improvisations. Just as the major scale has more melodic potential than its pentatonic cousin, the same is true of the aeolian mode when compared to the minor pentatonic. Deep Purple guitarist Ritchie Blackmore was one of the first rock guitarists to use the scale, in the early 1970s.

Amin7

Practice Notes: You won't achieve maximum benefit until you've transferred each example to the other four CAGED shapes. Once you can play the ideas fluently in all five shapes, transferring them to other keys is easy. In this way you are expanding both your harmonic and fingerboard knowledge. Example 1 is demanding, requiring both finger-rolling technique and extensive use of your fourth finger. Practice it ascending and descending and use alternate picking throughout. Example 2 is equally tricky, and also includes string skips between shapes—be sure to use the fingering indicated. Example 3 is a three-notes-per-string legato exercise—pick only the first note on each string ascending and descending. Example 4 is a string-bending exercise, climbing from the fourth fret of the third string to the fifteenth fret on the first string. Since it does not conform to any of the CAGED patterns, it can only be played in the one shape. Remember to use three fingers, bending with your third and using your first and second to add strength.

Emin7

Bmin7b5

Bmin7b5   **Cmaj7**   **Dmin7**

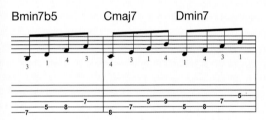

Fmaj7   **G7**   **Amin7**

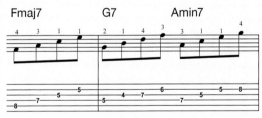

Cmaj7   **Bmin7b5**   **Amin7**   etc

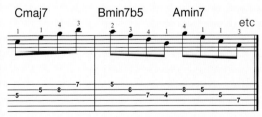

CHOPS BUILDER NO. 4:

AEOLIAN MODE CHOPS BUILDER

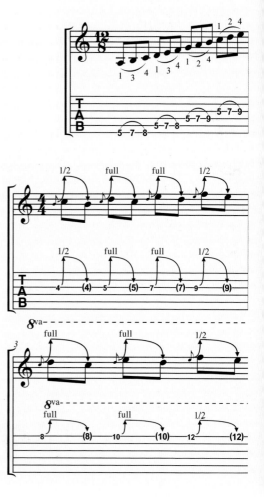

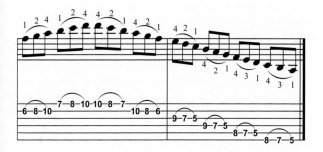

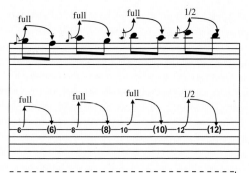

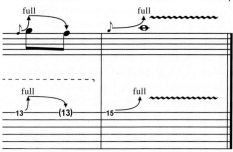

CHOPS BUILDER NO. 5:
MAJOR SEVENTH ARPEGGIOS

Arpeggio Type: 4-note, major seventh

Formulae: R–3–5–7

Usage: These two octave arpeggios have many applications. They can be played directly over a chord of the same root name (i.e., Cmaj7 arpeggio over a Cmaj7 chord) or superimposed over chords of a different quality and root name. Players of all styles use this technique to create exciting colors and tensions to their improvisations. Here are a couple of the most useful superimpositions and the color tones generated:

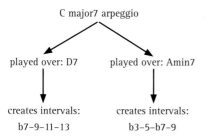

So to sum up, if you want to create dominant seventh sounds using a major seventh arpeggio, play it a tone below the dominant chord. To create minor sounds, play it a minor third (one and a half steps) above the minor chord.

Characteristics: The major seventh arpeggio is the most harmonically "stable" of all the seventh arpeggios. For this reason it is often superimposed

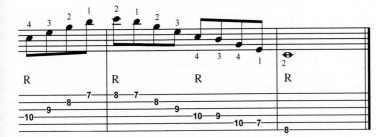

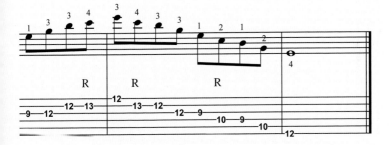

CHOPS BUILDER NO. 5:
MAJOR SEVENTH ARPEGGIOS

over minor and dominant chords, creating cool-sounding color tones with a solid harmonic structure.

Practice Notes: Position shifts and out of position stretches are common in all but examples 1 and 3. Use the suggested fingering for each shape and practice with alternate picking throughout. As with the scale shapes, root notes are highlighted between the staves with an "R" symbol. Once you're familiar with their location you should start memorizing where the remaining intervals are (3–5–7). To keep your ear up to speed, try singing the next note before you play it. You won't have enough vocal range to do this for all five shapes so just stick to a register that is comfortable for you. The accomplished improviser can hear phrases in their head before they play them—this obviously takes years of experience to realize, but you can accelerate your development with this simple technique (it works well with scales too!).

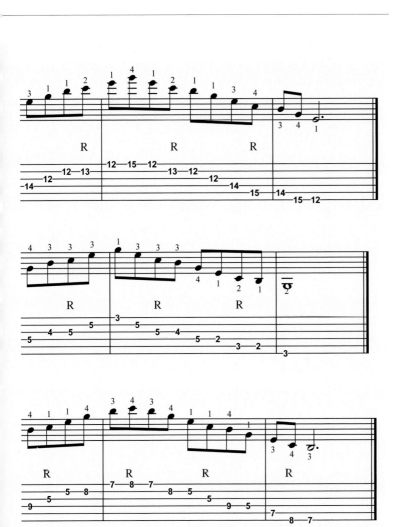

EQUIPMENT LIST

Guitarists always love talking and reading about the gear they use. So here's a list of all the guitars and equipment used to create the accompanying CD:

1975 Fender Telecaster
1979 Fender Stratocaster
1981 Gibson ES-175
1982 Gibson ES-335
2004 Fender Jazz Bass
2008 Gibson SG Bass
Little Labs Red Eye DI/Re-amp box
Palmer DI box with speaker simulator
Yamaha DG-1000 Guitar Pre-amp
Fulltone Clyde Deluxe Wah Wah
Native Instruments Guitar Rig 3

RECOMMENDED LISTENING

AC/DC, *Back in Black, Black Ice*
Chet Atkins, *Finger Style Guitar, Mister Guitar*
The Beatles, *Please Please Me, Sgt. Pepper's Lonely Hearts Club Band*
Chuck Berry, *After School Session, Berry is on Top*
Black Sabbath, *Volume Four, Sabotage*
Blur, *Blur*
Bon Jovi, *Slippery When Wet*
Boston, *Boston*
Eric Clapton, *461 Ocean Boulevard*
Cream, *Disraeli Gears, Goodbye Cream*
Steve Cropper (with Booker T. & The MGs), *Green Onions*
Deep Purple, *Deep Purple in Rock, Made in Japan*
Def Leppard, *Pyromania, Hysteria*

Derek And The Dominoes, *Layla and Other Assorted Love Songs*
The Foo Fighters, *One by One*
Free, *Fire and Water, The Free Story*
Rory Gallagher, *Irish Tour*
Genesis, *Selling England by the Pound, The Lamb Lies Down On Broadway*
Bill Haley, *Bill Haley and His Comets*
Uriah Heep, *Salisbury*
Iron Maiden, *The Number of the Beast*
Pat Martino, *Exit, Live at Yoshi's*
Metallica, *Master of Puppets*
Mountain, *Nantucket Sleighride*
Nirvana, *Bleach, Nevermind*
Oasis, *(What's the Story) Morning Glory?*
Pearl Jam, *Ten*

Pink Floyd, *Dark Side of the Moon, Wish You Were Here*
Elvis Presley, *Elvis Presley, Elvis is Back!*
Pulp, *Different Class*
Queen, *Sheer Heart Attack*
Radiohead, *The Bends*
Rage Against the Machine, *The Battle of Los Angeles*
REM, *Out of Time, Automatic for the People*
The Rolling Stones, *Sticky Fingers, Made in the Shade*
Soundgarden, *Superunknown*
Supergrass, *Supergrass*
Robin Trower, *Bridge of Sighs*
U2, *The Joshua Tree*
Van Halen, *Van Halen*
Whitesnake, *Ready an' Willing*
Yes, *The Yes Album, 90125*
ZZ Top, *Tres Hombres, Eliminator*

INDEX

PICTURE CREDITS

All musical notation, and the map on page 13, are © Quintet Publishing Limited. Other images are used with permission of the copyright holders named below (images are listed by page number). Fender®, Jazz Bass®, Telecaster®, Stratocaster®, and the distinctive headstock and body designs of the Fender® instruments depicted herein are trademarks of the Fender Musical Instruments Corporation and are used with permission.

2 Shutterstock; 7 Shutterstock; 11 Andrew Whittuck/Redferns; 12 RB/Redferns; 15 Diana Scrimgeour/ Redferns; 18-19 Shutterstock; 24 Shutterstock; 28 Shutterstock; 30 GAB Archives/Redferns; 32 Richi Howell/Redferns; 34 GAB Archives/Redferns; 36 Jan Persson/Redferns; 38 Ian Dickson/Rex Features; 40 CSU Archives/Everett Collection/Rex Features; 42 David Redfern/Redferns; 44 Bill Orchard/Rex Features; 46 Chris Foster/Rex Features; 48 GAB Archives/Redferns; 50 Ilpo Musto/Rex Features; 52 Robert Knight/Redferns; 54 Sipa Press/Rex Features; 56 David Redfern/Redferns; 58 Shutterstock; 60 Andrew Lepley/Redferns; 62 K&K Ulf Kruger Ohg/Redferns; 64 Rex/Christies Images Ltd.2008; 66 David Redfern/Redferns; 68 Pictorial Press Ltd/Alamy; 70 Colin Fuller/Redferns; 72 GAB Archives/ Redferns; 74 Dezo Hoffmann/Rex Features; 76 GAB Archives/Redferns; 78 Andre Csillag/Rex Features; 80 ITV/Rex Features; 82 GAB Archives/Redferns; 84 Graham Lowe/Redferns; 86 Robert Knight/Redferns; 88 GAB Archives/Redferns; 90 Elliott Landy, Landyvision, Inc./Digimarc; 92 GAB Archives/Redferns; 94 BOB KING/Redferns; 96 Jorgen Angel/Redferns; 98 Rob Verhorst/Redferns; 100 GAB Archives/Redferns; 102 GAB Archives/Redferns; 104 Ed Perlstein/Redferns; 106 GAB Archives/ Redferns; 108 Ed Perlstein/Redferns; 110 GAB Archives/Redferns; 112 Alain Dister/APRF; 114 Gilles Petard Collection/Redfe; 116 Redferns/Redferns; 118 Elliott Landy, Landyvision, Inc/Digimarc; 120 Tony Kyriacou/Rex Features; 122 GAB Archives/Redferns; 124 David Corio; 126 Fin Costello/Redferns; 128 Ebet Roberts/Redferns; 130 John Lynn Kirk/Redferns; 132 Richard E Aaron/Redferns; 134 Phil Dent/Redferns; 136 Redferns/Redferns; 138 GAB Archives/Redferns; 140 GAB Archives/Redferns; 142 Fin Costello/Redferns; 144 Mick Hutson/ Redferns; 146 Jan Persson/Redferns; 148 GAB Archives/ Redferns; 150 Andrew Putler/Redferns; 152 GAB Archives/Redferns; 154 GAB Archives/Redferns; 156 GAB Archives/Redferns; 158 Peter Sanders/Redferns; 160 GAB Archives/Redferns; 162 Jan Persson/ Redferns; 164 Paul Bergen/Redferns; 166 Ebet Roberts/Redferns; 168 Fin Costello/ Redferns; 170 GAB Archives/Redferns; 172 Fin Costello/Redferns; 174 Fin Costello/Redferns; 176 John Livzey/ Redferns; 180 Richard E. Aaron/Rockpix; 182 Ebet Roberts/Redferns; 184 George Chin/Redferns; 186 Richard E Aaron/Redferns; 188 Phil Dent/Redferns; 190 Mike Cameron/Redferns; 192 Carey Brandon/ Redferns; 194 Paul Bergen/Redferns; 196 Neil Lupin/Redferns; 198 Michel Linssen/Redferns; 200 Paul Bergen/Redferns; 202 JJ Gonson/Redferns; 204 GAB Archives/Redferns; 206 George Chin/ Redferns; 208 Mick Hutson/Redferns; 208 Rob Verhorst/Redferns; 212 Paul Bergen/Redferns; 214 Shutterstock; 252 Fender Musical Instruments Corporation.